Bedfordshire Lace Designs

LOUISE WEST

Published by Louise West Lace Design

ISBN 978 0 9957370 0 6

Printed by Short Run Press Ltd, Exeter, Devon

Thank you to . . .

Margaret Tite for introducing me to Bedfordshire lace and for persuading me to persist with it when initially I felt it was not for me.

Barbara Underwood for inspiring me and motivating me through many Thomas Lester designs, sparking a fascination in the complicated Art Nouveau style designs, and for starting me on my design journey.

Anita Wilkinson for many years of classes, support and setting challenges, all of which added to my knowledge and thirst for designing.

The BA tutors at the University of Derby for making me believe anything is possible, and to the MA for developing my direction with lace.

Many other teachers who I have done occasional classes or workshops with. You have all added to my education with lace, and helped in many ways.

Katy White for working pieces, checking the technical diagrams and visual proof reading, and for being happy to try out new designs when I needed someone to test them.

Victoria Brown for allowing use of her art as inspiration for a design.

Laurie Waters for allowing use of a piece of lace in her collection.

Gwynedd Roberts for the introduction.

Ann Day for reviewing the book.

Ewan Mathers for the photography.

Elliot Davies for proof reading.

To the many students who have prompted me to write the book, asking for new designs to work.

And for the support from around the world in encouraging me to continue working on the designs in this book, at times when it felt like it was never going to be finished. The lace world is more connected thanks to social media.

And finally to everyone reading and working the patterns. I hope you enjoy all of these Bedfordshire designs.

FOREWORD

The designs in this book have been inspired by a range of sources, some historical, others from plant life, and one from another artist's painting. All sources are used with permission of either the owner of the lace or the art, and where appropriate the source is credited. All the pieces are worked by the author or credited to the lacemaker who worked the design.

The book is not aimed at the complete beginner to lacemaking, but at the lacemaker who has some knowledge of Bedfordshire who wants to work new patterns. The patterns grow progressively more difficult through the book, and although instructions are given for the early patterns, less instruction is given later as the difficulty increases. For many of the floral patterns, it is up to the lacemaker as to the number of pairs added to fill cloth stitch areas, and so only a guide as to the number of pairs required is given. This will vary between individual lacemakers, depending on thread, tension and individual preference to the density of the lace. But it should be remembered that Bedfordshire lace should be fairly solid. It was a heavier lace, designed to be bolder during the 19th century to suit the fashion of the time.

The patterns in this book have all been worked in varying thicknesses of Presencia Finca threads which the author finds to be one of the most pleasing for Bedfordshire lace. It gives a clean and crisp finish straight off the lace pillow. Other threads can be substituted in suitable equivalent thicknesses. The threads stated are what the examples were made with, and the finish may vary slightly if alternatives are used. This is not a fault with the thread, the lacemaker, or the pattern, but a characteristic of handmade lace. Embrace this and enjoy working the patterns.

Note – To aid clarity, the patterns are printed in black and the working diagrams are printed in colour. The colours do not signify anything. They are only used to distinguish between the threads. They are not related to any other code in lacemaking.

INTRODUCTION

There are three unique bobbin laces associated with the English East Midlands counties of Buckinghamshire, Northamptonshire and Bedfordshire. Whilst the first two developed from laces brought to England from areas in Western Europe, the tradition is that the latter lace was influenced by the Maltese silk guipure laces shown at The Great Exhibition in 1851. Indeed, well into the 20th century it was known as Bedfordshire Maltese, despite the fact that it was not necessarily made in that county! Other influences are the French Cluny and Le Puy guipure laces particularly as the 19th century progressed, nor should we forget the part that the lacemakers themselves had on the technique, as prior to being called upon to work this new style of lace, they had been making fine grounded laces such as Mechlin and Buckinghamshire Point. The 60+ years that this guipure lace was extensively made by the professional lacemakers of the East Midlands, gave time for a distinctive set of techniques to develop.

By the start of the First World War, the industry was in serious decline, and the patterns had become coarse and showing limited variation in design. It was this basic form of Bedfordshire (or Beds. as many call it) that was taught to the amateur lacemakers of the 1950-70's when there was a resurgence of awareness in the skills of bobbin lacemaking. These new lacemakers were making lace for enjoyment, and they wanted interesting patterns. They started looking at old prickings and finished laces in Museums and private collections, and discovered that the earlier Beds. designs of the 19th century were vastly superior in design to most of those they had inherited from the early 20th century. The name of Thomas Lester became synonymous with these complex designs, but he of course was not the only Dealer to be producing such work, the provenance of much of which still remains unknown.

In 1986 when Margaret Turner produced her book "Bedfordshire Lace Patterns" it was an eye opener to many who had not appreciated the complexity and beauty of the older form of Beds. This book was a collection of old prickings, not all of which had a photo of the finished piece, plus a brief comment. Around this time Ann Day and Margaret Tite investigated the V & A collection of the Prickings of the Dealer known as "Sargeant of Sandy" and eventually two books of these "Advanced Bedfordshire Patterns" were published by the Lace Guild. Several Instruction books concentrating on the basic techniques were published in this era, but direct tuition on lace courses was the principal way by which the knowledge of the advanced techniques was passed on. In 1988 the first book to cover this in depth, Barbara Underwood's "Traditional Bedfordshire Lace- techniques and patterns", allowed the knowledge about this wonderful lace to spread world-wide.

The 21st century lacemaker does not necessarily wish to spend hours working repetitive patterns. Some do not wish to wear the lace they have made, as their pleasure comes from the activity of making it. They work to achieve the best quality of work that they can, so speed of working is secondary. Today's makers are proud of their work and their achievement, so many beautify their homes by hanging it as a picture on the wall, where it can be seen by all.

As a lace designer and maker, Louise West is inspired by the floral designs to be found in the prickings from the golden age of Beds., when Victorian fashions demanded quality designs, and the incorporation of realistic flowers and leaves let alone butterflies were popular themes. The original Prickings for large Collars, Capes, Falling caps, Lappets, Ties, Parasol covers and other pieces for the embellishment of clothing, may hold little interest for working as inherited, but their design ideas and motifs can, as is shown in this book, be put into a new context in a manageable size to be undertaken in a reasonable timescale. Other of the patterns in this book are Louise's own inspiration, thus bringing new shapes and forms into play. It is important that although we might learn from the past, that new designs such as these do get devised in the present, so that the future of this special lace technique is assured.

Gwynedd H Roberts

Hon. Curator
The Lace Guild

1

BOOKMARK

Made in Presencia Finca 60 thread and 28 pairs of bobbins. Any equivalent thread can be substituted.

This bookmark was designed as a starting point for lacemakers fairly new to Bedfordshire lace, but with some experience of lacemaking techniques. It assumes knowledge of making leaf tallies and plaits.

It contains techniques of leaf tallies, trails, plaits, windmill crossings and eight pair crossings.

Colouring in pricking

This is particularly useful when working patterns of Bedfordshire lace, as it helps the lacemaker work out which pin holes belong to which area of cloth stitch or other adjacent elements. If you are unsure if you will like the design, photocopy the pattern first and colour in areas of cloth stitch to help you visualise what the lace will look like. The pens used should be permanent and waterproof. Brush pens work well, but ensure they are permanent for use on the actual pricking.

This technique was introduced to students at Barbara Underwood's courses. The technique was also used by 20th century designer Amy Atkins in her designs for the Nottingham lace industry between 1904 and 1914. The drawings are now housed at Newstead Abbey in the lace archives belonging to the Nottingham City Council (UK).

Working diagram 1 - showing start and where pairs are added.

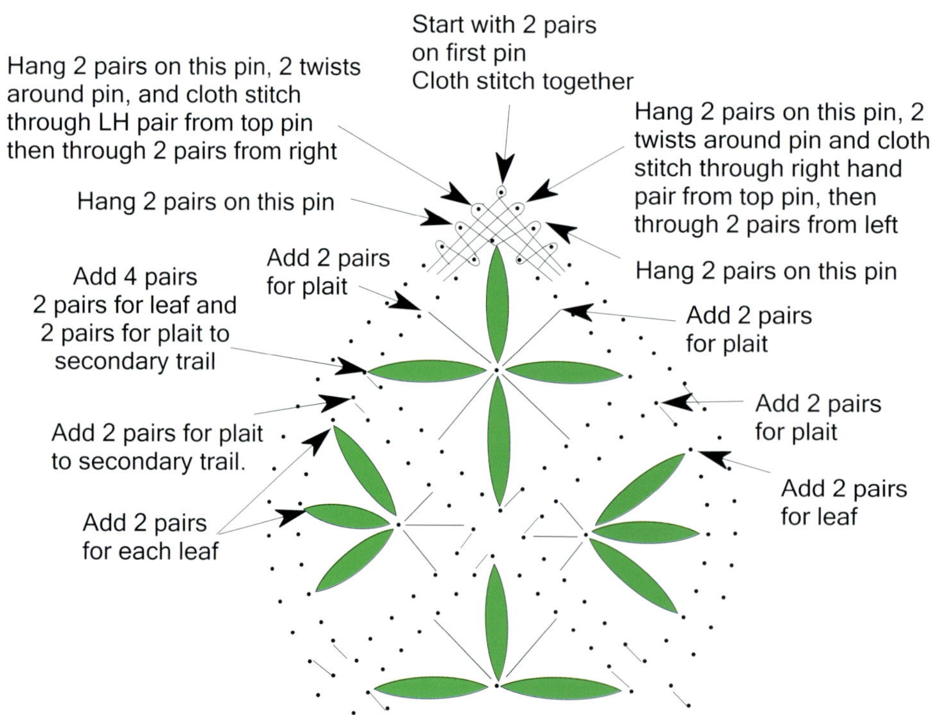

To start this bookmark, the two pairs are hung on the first pin, in open formation and with one pair twisted twice.

Cloth stitch the two pairs together.

For the next two pins (left and right) hang two pairs on and twist one pair twice on each.

Cloth stitch pairs from the left pin, through the left hand pair from the top pin.

Cloth stitch the pairs from the right pin through the right hand pair from the top pin.

Cloth stitch the two left hand pairs from the second pin, through the two right hand pairs from the second pin. This means you now have three pairs of passives for each trail, and they have cloth stitch through each other to form the top inverted V shape point.

The next two pins on each side also have two pairs hung on them in the same manner, in open formation and with one pair twisted twice. The first pair from each side cloth stitches through the three passives, meets with a pair from other side, and cloth stitches together at the central pin to become the leaf. The second pair from this pin becomes the worker for the trail.

This pattern features the use of primary and secondary trails. The secondary trails start with the two plaits being left out from the primary or main trail. By working the two pairs as a plait to start the trail, the secondary trail appears to emerge from behind the main trail, deceiving the eye into believing it is three dimensional. A similar effect is seen in Celtic knots. It is a useful technique that helps Bedfordshire become more alive than just a flat piece of lace.

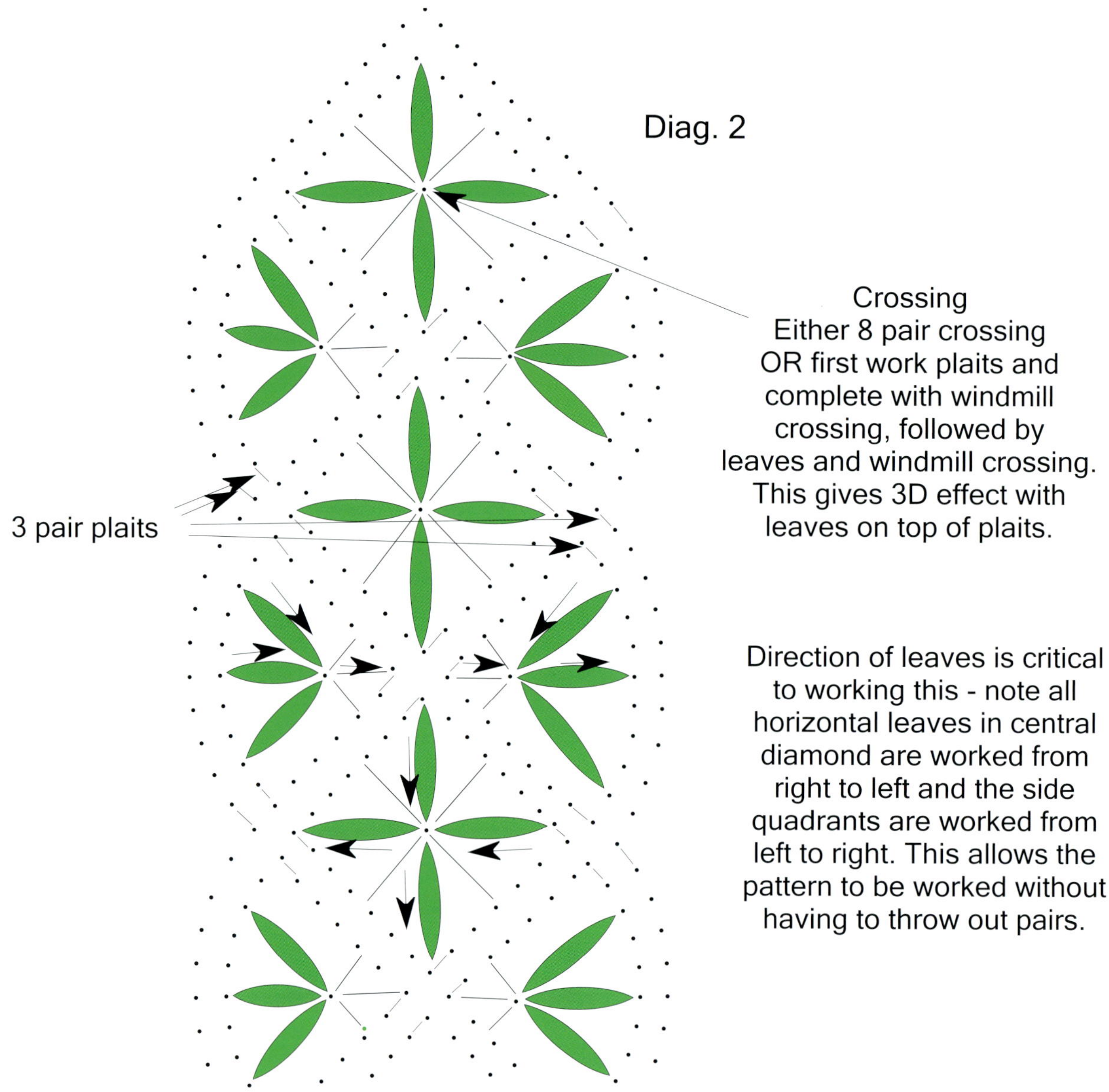

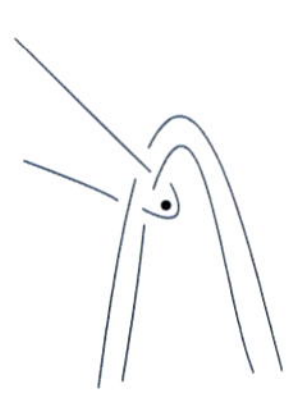

Adding pairs

Hang the new pairs on a temporary support pin near to where they are required. Using worker from trail, work through the first pair (if 2 pairs are being added) and put pin in the hole where the plait/leaf needs to come from.

This ensures that the added pairs are around the pin as shown in the diagram.

Four pair windmill crossing

A windmill crossing is worked with four pairs of bobbins, from plaits, leaves, or a combination of both. Each pair of bobbins is treated as a single bobbin and a cloth stitch is worked, with the pin being put in before the last move, the last two over three.

Eight pair crossing

This crossing is done with eight pairs of bobbins, either from plaits, leaves, or a combination of both as in this pattern.

Each pair of bobbins is treated as a single thread throughout.

1. With the centre four pairs, work a half stitch.
2. With the right hand four pairs, work a half stitch
3. With the left hand four pairs, work a half stitch

Repeat these three steps once more

Put up pin

With the centre four pairs, work a cloth stitch, and then two over three and six over seven to complete.

Written in shorter form:

Count the bobbins from the left, numbering 1, 2, 3, 4, 5, 6, 7, and 8

4 over 5; 4 over 3; 6 over 5; 6 over 7; 6 over 5; 8 over 7; 2 over 3; 2 over 1; 4 over 3. Repeat this once more and then pin in the centre.

Then 4 over 5; 4 over 3; 6 over 5; 4 over 5; 2 over 3; 6 over 7.

Three pair plaits

These plaits are worked using three pairs.

Start at one side – it can be the left or the right, but continue from this side throughout the plait.

Put one twist on the first pair you are starting with, cloth stitch through the two pairs, and twist once again.

Start back at the same side as the first time and repeat, each time starting from either the left or right.

Work until the plait is long enough.

In some patterns three pairs are not required in the next element. In this case, a pair can be thrown out during the plait.

Finishing the bookmark

As the bookmark becomes narrower, more pairs are taken into the outside trail and have to be thrown out to maintain the width of the trail. When throwing pairs out, throw out alternate threads rather than ones next to each other, reducing the risk of a hole being left where they are taken out. To throw out, lengthen the thread and lay the bobbins to the back of the pillow. Always throw out pairs that have been in the trail the longest, and take care not to pull the ones laid to the back.

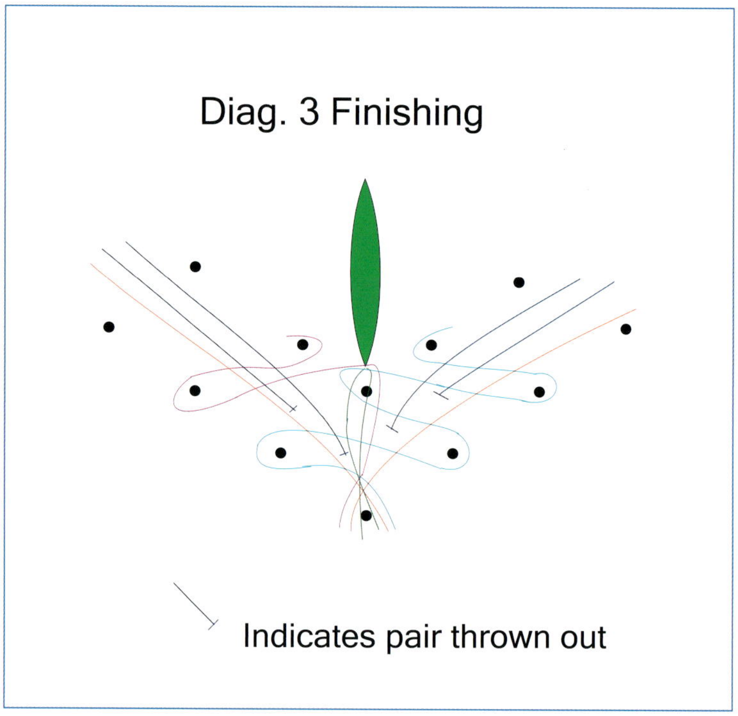

Maintain three pairs of passives until the two trails meet. On reaching the last vertical leaf (the two workers meet at the central pin), take one pair from the leaf into each trail, before cloth stitching the two workers together and putting up the pin. The left hand worker then works across to the right side and then back across all the passives to the left side. The two trails are now one trail of cloth stitch. On each of the rows, a pair can be thrown out. On reaching the last central pin hole, a pin is put up in the centre of the remaining pairs, and then a plait is worked with the remaining bobbins divided into four groups. The pairs are used as if they are single bobbins and plaited for however long the plait is needed.

2

Leaves Bookmark

Made in Presencia Finca 60 thread, approximately 64 pairs.

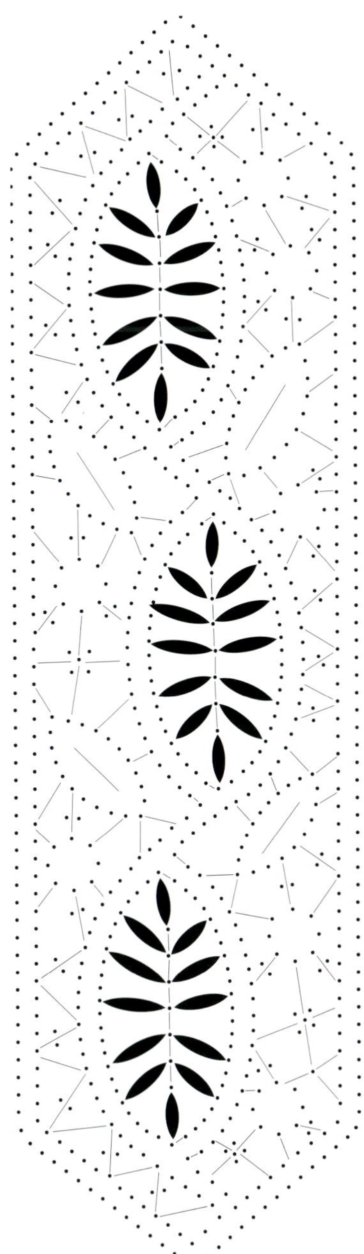

Lace made by Katy White

Additional techniques to first bookmark: picots, Bedfordshire half stitch buds, and leaves with twisted central veins.

This pattern is becoming more floral, with pairs added in and thrown out when no longer required. This happens during the working of the small side leaves that have a line marked indicating a central vein. The vein is worked by twisting the worker on each row as it crosses the vertical line down the centre of the leaf. Two or three twists can be used, depending on how large a vein is required.

To throw out a pair in cloth stitch, do not take two bobbins that are next to each other. Take out alternate bobbins to make the pair thrown out less noticeable in the resulting lace.

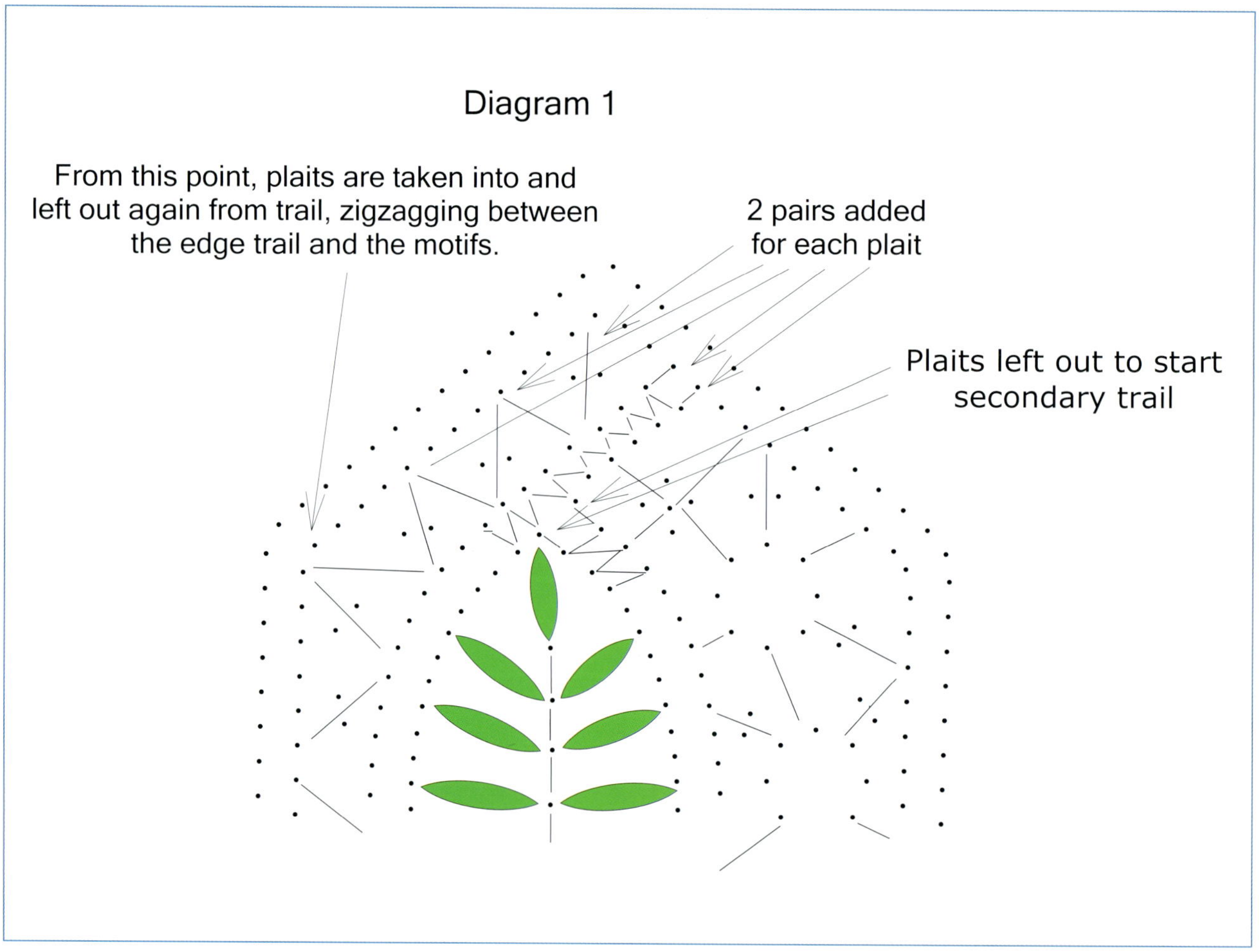

The pattern is started with the trail in the same way as the first bookmark.

Many Bedfordshire patterns, including some of the designs in this book, show markings for plaits drawn in between two pinholes. This sometimes confuses lacemakers who are new to Bedfordshire. However, Bedfordshire lace is often about making decisions yourself as to how you want the lace to look. Where a plait is drawn between two pinholes, it means that it can come from either pin hole depending on how it looks when you work it. The line means 'around this pinhole, there is a plait' and NOT 'at this pinhole there MUST be a plait'. This

is a subtle yet important difference. Quite often the plaited ground will lay between pin holes. It is up to you to decide at the time which one will give the most accurate look to the ground. This will vary depending on how accurately the pricking has been prepared.

Finishing the bookmark

This design can be finished in the same way as bookmark 1. But if you do not want a plait, it can also be finished by joining the trails. Ideally join the trails off centre, so that the eye is not drawn towards the finish, making it easier to hide it.

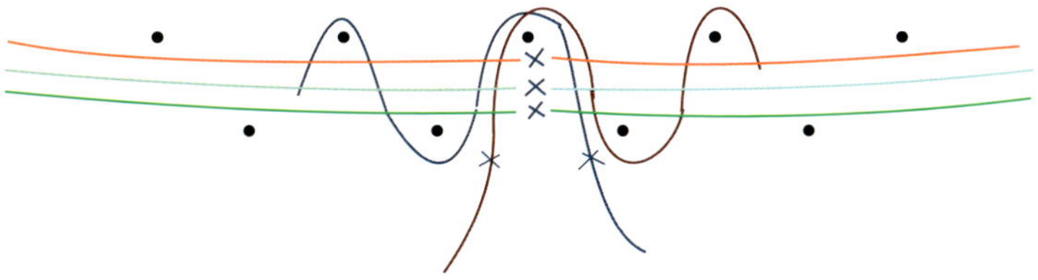

Diagram 2 Joining two trails to finish

Cloth stitch the workers together at the last pin on the inside edge, and then back out through the passives to outside.
The passives are then tied in a reef knot, taking one bobbin from each side to tie the knot with, starting at the inside, (shown orange on diagram) tying each pair in turn.
Lastly tie the two pairs of workers
All the ends can then be taken through to the back to fasten off.

3

Simple Hexagon Edging

Made in Presencia Finca 60 and 24 pairs of bobbins.

Lace made by Katy White

Edgings are worked with the footside on the right and headside on the left in Bedfordshire lace.

Techniques used include pairs entering the trail and passives exiting to form a sharp point on the trail. The trail on the headside edge maintains a minimum of three pairs of passives plus a worker. The footside is worked with two passives, a worker and edge pair.

This design also has an eight pair crossing that offers the opportunity to use the alternative crossing to the one used on pattern 1.

The six leaf shaped tallies on the outside edge that form a flower-like shape are worked as three leaf shaped tallies and then a six pair crossing, followed by three further leaf shaped tallies. They look slightly different to other leaf shaped tallies connected with this crossing as they are all to one side of the pin, which gives them their flower-like appearance.

Starting the edging

Start with three passives and a worker pair at the highest pin on the outside edge, marked with O. The pairs are hung side by side on a support pin to the back of the work to start. Once two rows have been worked (adding in the pairs at the pin marked * for the two plaits), the support pin can be laid flat on the pillow, behind the two first pins. This keeps the loops that will be needed to join the trail at the finish. It should be possible to see the individual loops of the pairs over the pin, side by side. Continue to add pairs as marked on the diagram, also starting the footside in the same manner.

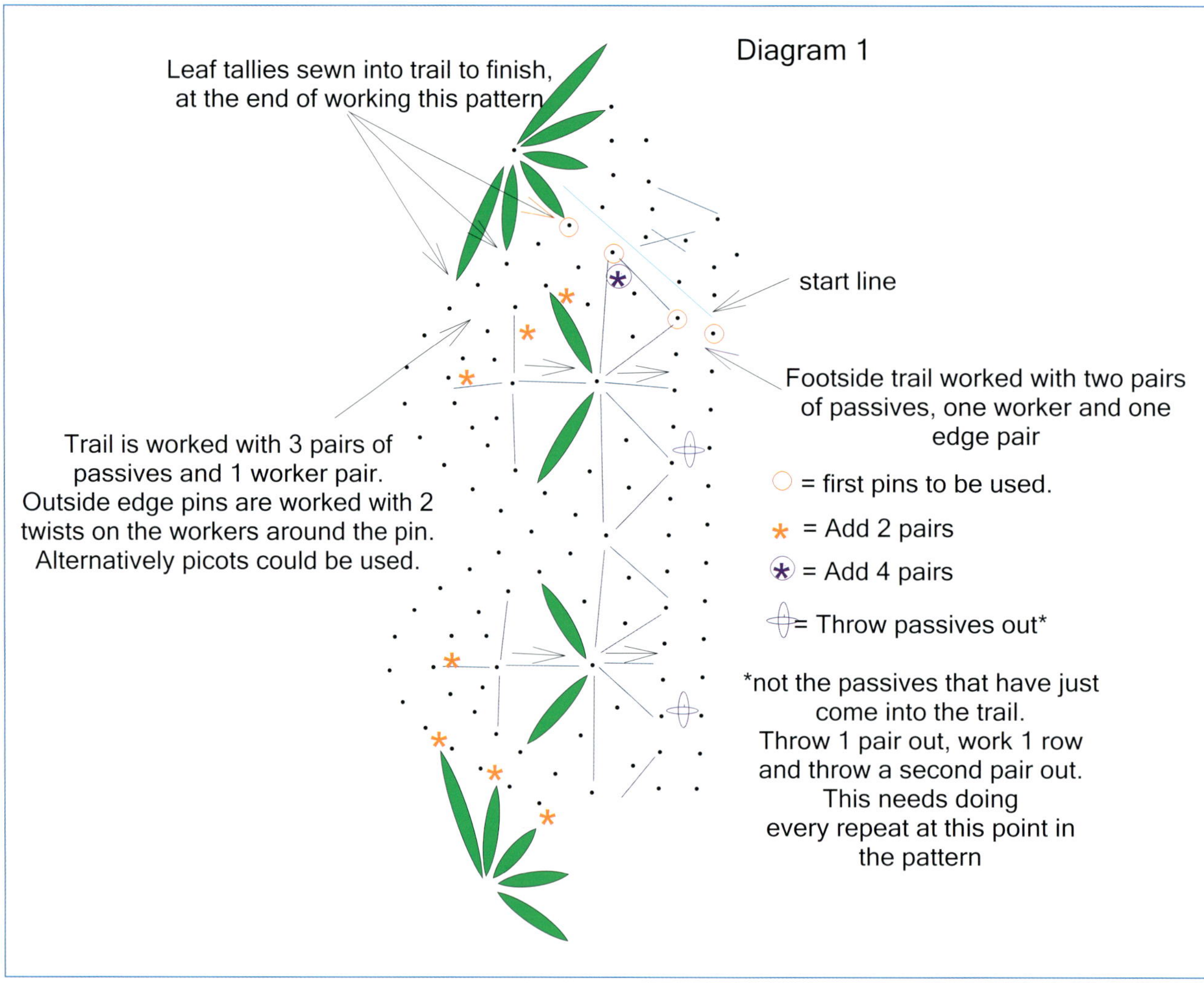

Working the sharp point of the trail

The worker is left at the pin on the inside of the V, on the left side of this pattern, while the point is worked. As the diagram shows, there should be three pins on the outside that are as yet unworked. There are two plaits coming into the trail.

The first plait, place a pin at the end of the plait, between the two pairs of each plait. Cloth stitch two passives through the first plait.

Then with the second plait, cloth stitch the two passive pairs of the trail through three of the four plait pairs.

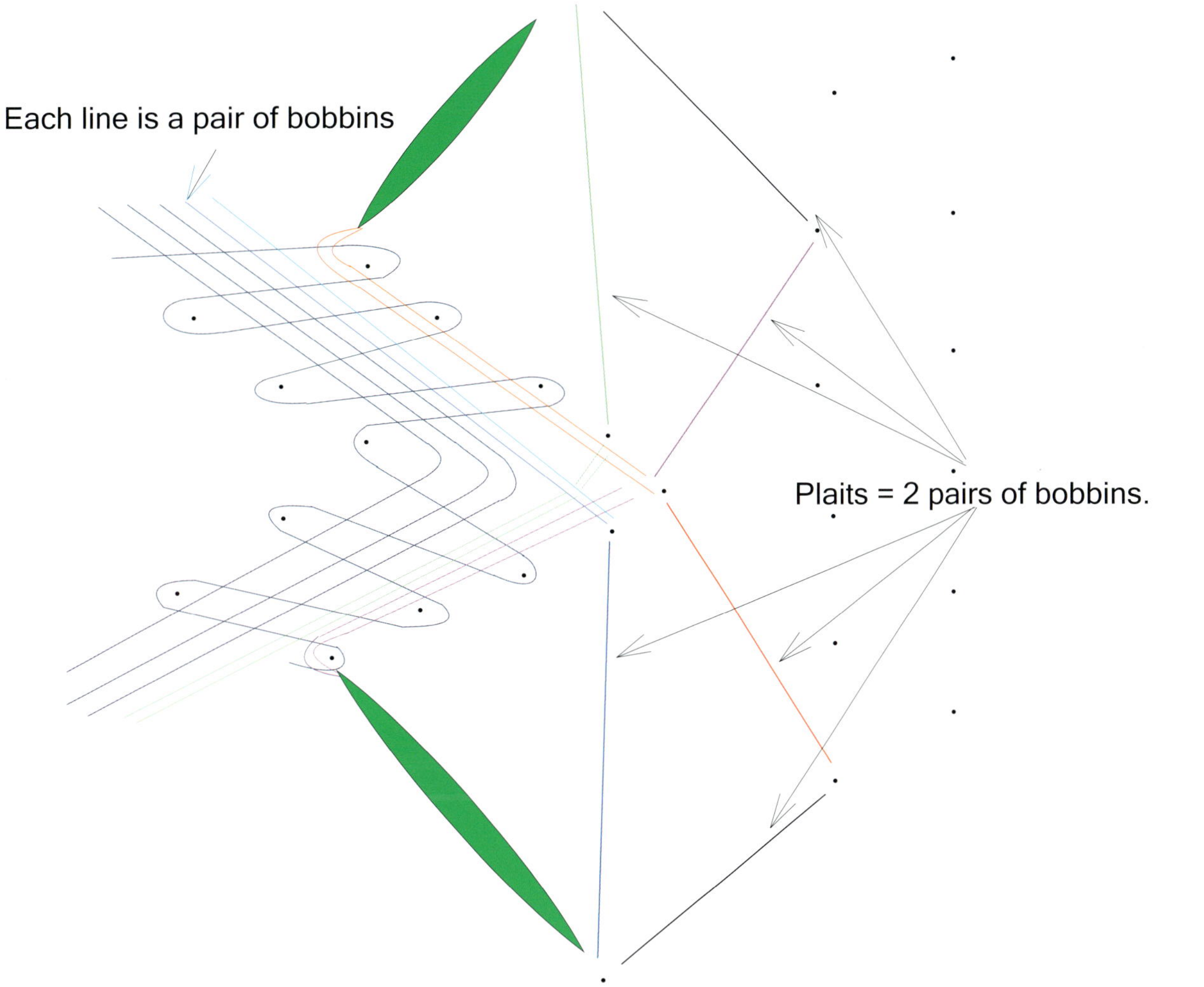

At the sharp point of the trail, where the pairs enter the trail from the plaits, cloth stitch the plait pairs through the next 4 pairs of the trail passives, the passives exit the trail to become the plaits. Pin is inserted before the last cloth stitch is worked at the point, ensuring that the pin is covered by the last stitch.

Pin at the point and then cloth stitch the last one through. These two passive pairs become the plait leaving the trail.

The next two trail passive pairs work through the original four plait pairs to become the next plait exiting the trail. The original plait pairs have now changed places with the passives and become the passives in the trail to continue.

Finishing

On completing the edging, the ends need joining into the start.

The trail passives and workers are 'sewn' in to the loops left on the pin laying horizontally at the back of the first pins. This can be done with a very fine crotchet hook, though this is a fiddly process that can split threads on fine lace. So instead use a Lazy Susan, or an eyes out tool. This tool allows the threads on the bobbins to be pulled through the loops before they are knotted using the reef knot.

There has been much debate over the years as to whether you should leave the lace on the pillow to "set". It is a personal choice whether you do this. But consider the lacemakers of the 19th century and earlier. They would make lace by the yard, and they did not have the luxury of leaving pins in for 24 hours or more – all without a noticeable effect. It may have been influenced by the type of threads they were using. Earlier lacemakers used linen, and the change to cotton bought about changes to how it worked. Or perhaps the conditions in the unheated and probably damp cottages meant that the lace did not need to "set". However, today's lacemakers do not have to contend with the pressures of the 19th century, and so we have a choice. No harm will come to the lace being left for 24 hours, though it is debatable whether you will be able to tell the difference if it is removed straight after finishing. Most of the pins will have been in the pillow for more than 24 hours anyway. It is only the last few you use that will not have been.

4

SNOWFLAKE

Made in Presencia Finca 60 with 34 pairs.

This snowflake design can be worked around the motif, as if working a round edging. The central trail is worked leaving out pairs for the first three leaf tallies. When the three leaves can be worked, make the leaf tallies and immediately do the six pair crossing to secure the leaf tallies.

For the more experienced worker using more pairs, it can be worked from top to bottom. This is how it was worked in the photograph. Though the overall effect is the same, the pattern will look slightly different to a pattern that has been worked in the round. For less experienced lacemakers, work this design around the motif.

The trails surrounding the leaf tally sprays are started by laying pairs in, in both directions, using the two pairs from a plait as the starting point. The two pairs from the plait become the workers, one to go to the right and one to the left.

Note – where the trail goes beyond the round outline, the pins on the edge are worked as picots.

Diagram 1 Starting a trail in both directions

For the start of this piece, hang 2 pairs on this pin and twist 1 of the pairs twice. (in subsequent repeats these 2 pairs will be from a plait)

Hang 6 pairs on temporary support pin (this is in open formation)

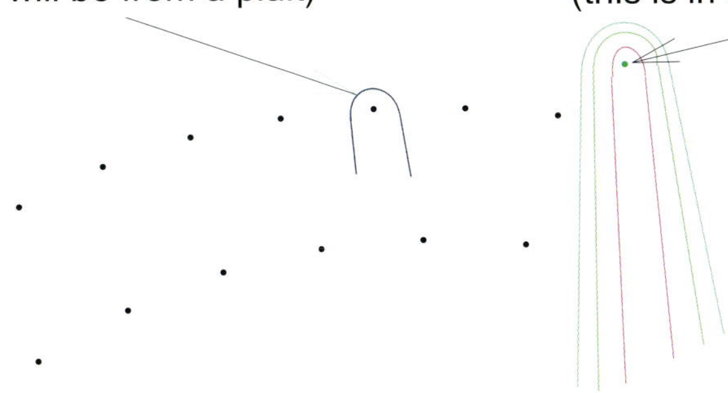

The 2 pairs hung on the pin in the trail will become the workers, with 1 pair working the left hand side and 1 pair working the right. The 6 pairs hung on the temporary support pin will become passives in both directions of the trail.

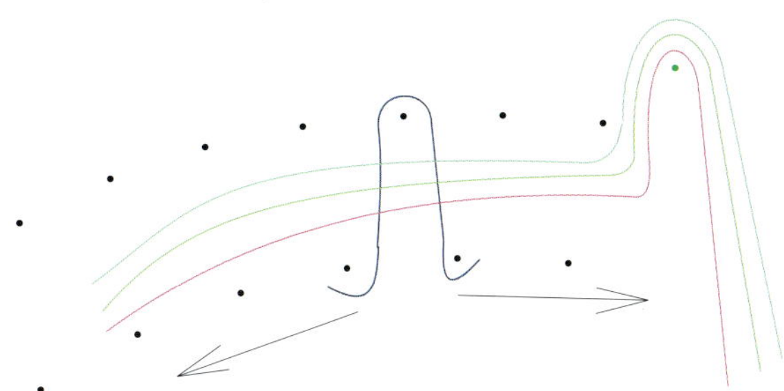

Work both pairs of workers through the first 3 pairs hung on the support pin (these will be the passives for the left trail). Pin the next 2 pins as shown.
Once these 2 pins have been put in, the temporary support pin can be removed.

The trail is now started in both directions

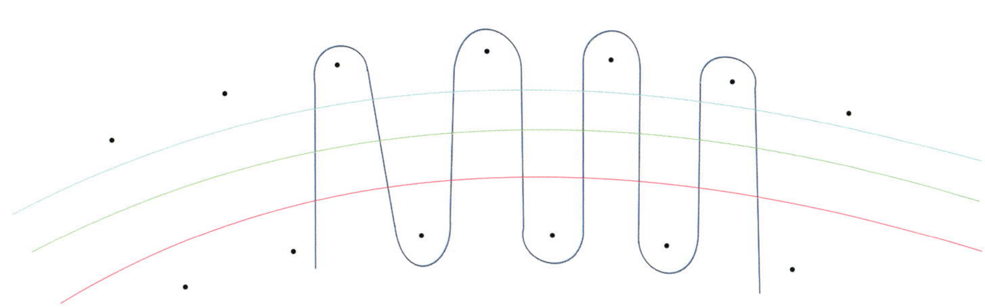

Closing the oval trails

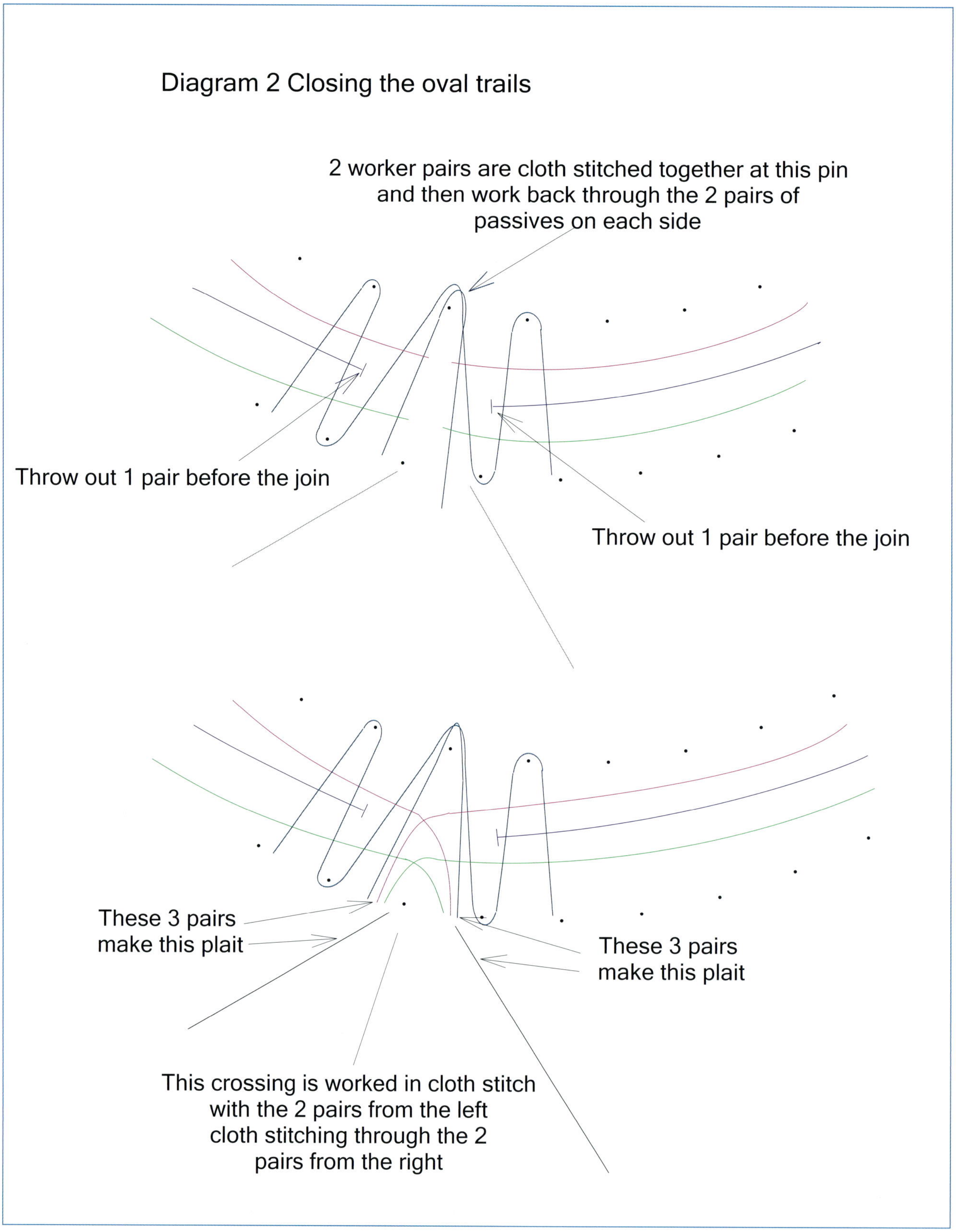

The half stitch circles, the Bedfordshire buds, have raised and rolled tallies worked on top of the half stitch. The tallies are worked when the half stitch circle is half way.

Six pair crossing

The six leaves inside the central trail use a six pair crossing.

Three leaves are worked and then the crossing is made.

Using all the pairs as a single, work the following:

Count the bobbins from the left, numbering 1, 2, 3, 4, 5, and 6.

2 over 3; 4 over 5; 4 over 3; 2 over 3; 2 over 1; 4 over 5; 6 over 5; PIN.

2 over 3; 4 over 5; 4 over 3; 2 over 3; 4 over 5.

5

DIAMONDS AND LEAVES EDGING

Made in Presencia Finca 60.

This little edging is designed to give practice for those who do not like leaf tallies. It does, however, feature a few other techniques, including practice at six pair crossing, and trails crossing.

This design takes 22 pairs for the edging and a further 10 pairs for the corner. The pairs are put in to work the corner and then thrown out as the corner ends.

Starting the edging

Diagram 1

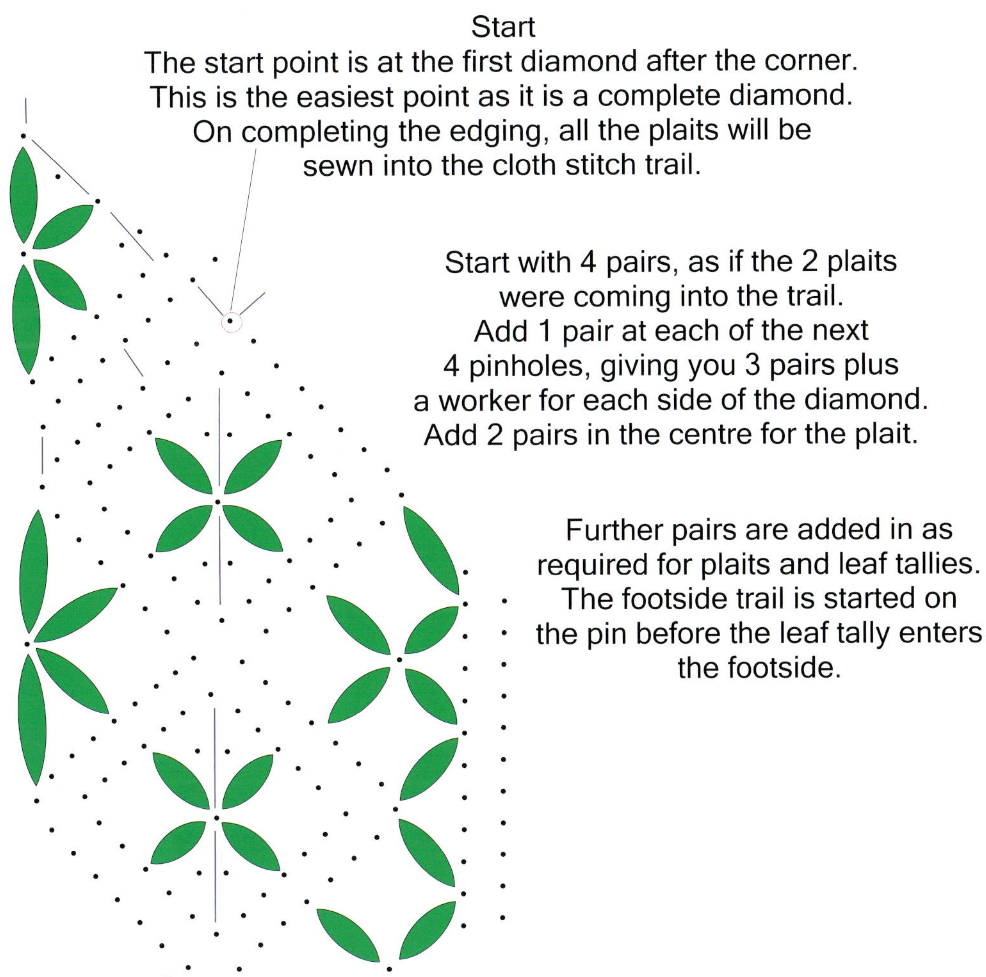

Crossing trails

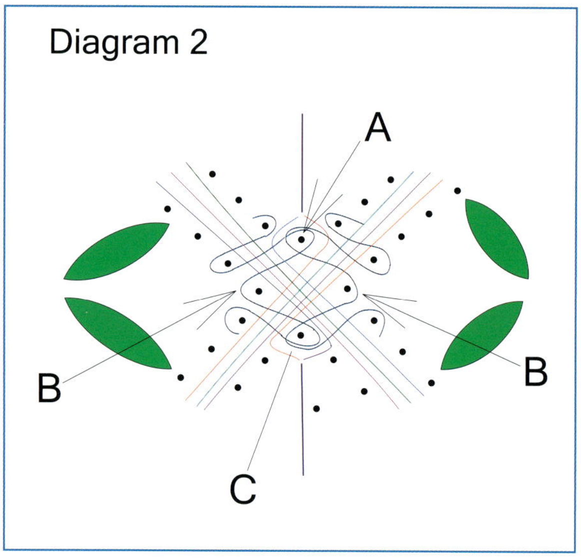

The plait is entering the trail at pin A.

Take one pair from the plait into the left trail and one into the right trail.

The two workers then meet at pin A, cloth stitch together and then work back to pin B.

The workers are left at the sides (at pin B), while the passives on the left trail cloth stitch through the passives on the right trail.

The workers then cloth stitch back through the passives to meet again at pin C.

Cloth stitch them together, pin, and then return to their respective trails, leaving one pair of passives out from each side to form the plait.

Corner

Ten extra pairs are required to work the corner, which are then thrown out when the corner has been worked.

The working diagram of the corner shows the direction of the plaits and leaf tallies. It also shows where pairs need adding in.

Diagram 3

* Pairs need throwing out to reduce the number to 4 pairs at the end of the diamond. The 4 pairs then make the 2 plaits

Corner trail starts here
Add 2 pairs on a temporary support pin to the side and work a windmill crossing with the 2 pairs from the plait to start.

◯ Pins where 2 pairs are added

◯ Pins where 1 pair is added

This segment is worked in the same direction as the edging before turning the work 90 degrees to continue

* Throw out pairs towards the end of the trail to leave 3 pairs in the plait. Throw 1 more pair out during the plait

6

FOUR LEAF CLOVER MOTIF

Design source: Machine lace in dealer's pattern book, from Nottingham Lace industry of Thomas Stocks, held in private collection of Victoria Brown.

Many pieces of historical machine lace can give inspiration for new designs. Designers for the machine lace industry took inspiration from handmade designs. But just like the designers of today, they were also influenced by the fashions and styles of the time. Many modern lacemakers do not like to sit at one design for months, making long lengths with multiple repeats. Instead, most like to smaller pieces which is why motifs are often more popular than traditional edgings.

Made in Presencia Finca 60 and approximately 60-70 pairs of bobbins.

Lace worked by Katy White.

Repeating elements within a piece of lace gives the lacemaker more experience to fully understand how the piece works, particularly when first learning a new style of lace. This design offers four repeats within the motif to give a little practice of the elements it contains.

Starting the motif

As detailed in pattern 4, the motif is started by setting in the trail in both directions on the oval shape surrounding the star trail. Pairs are added as indicated for the plaits.

The star trail

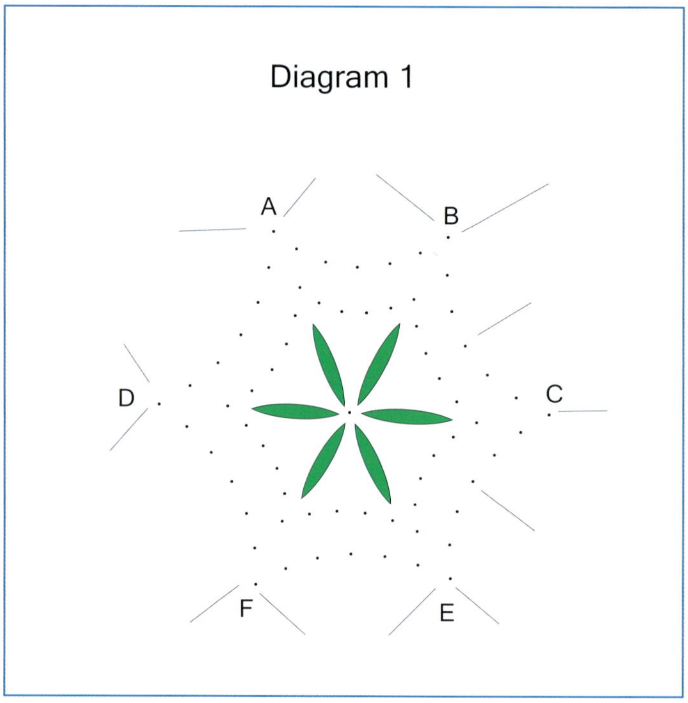

The start at Pin A

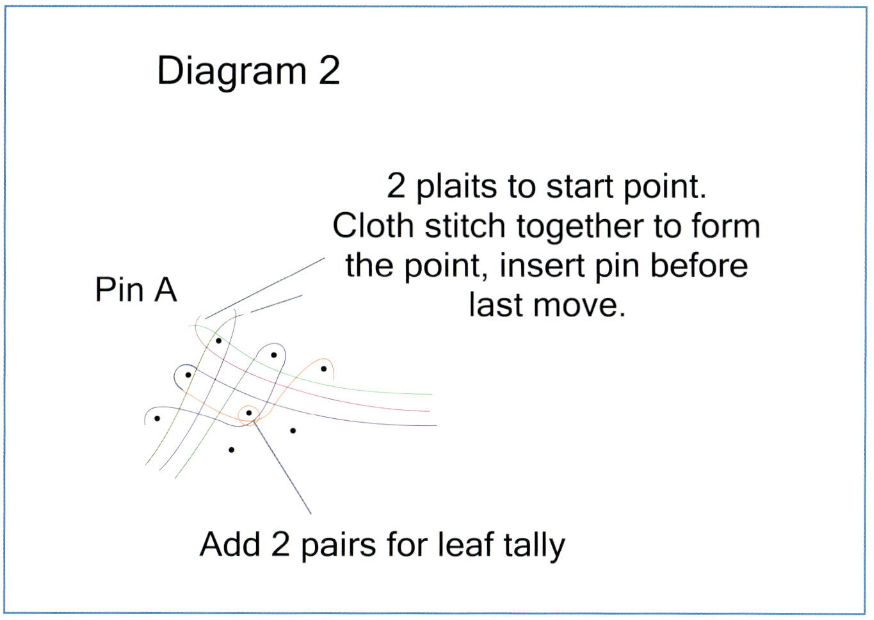

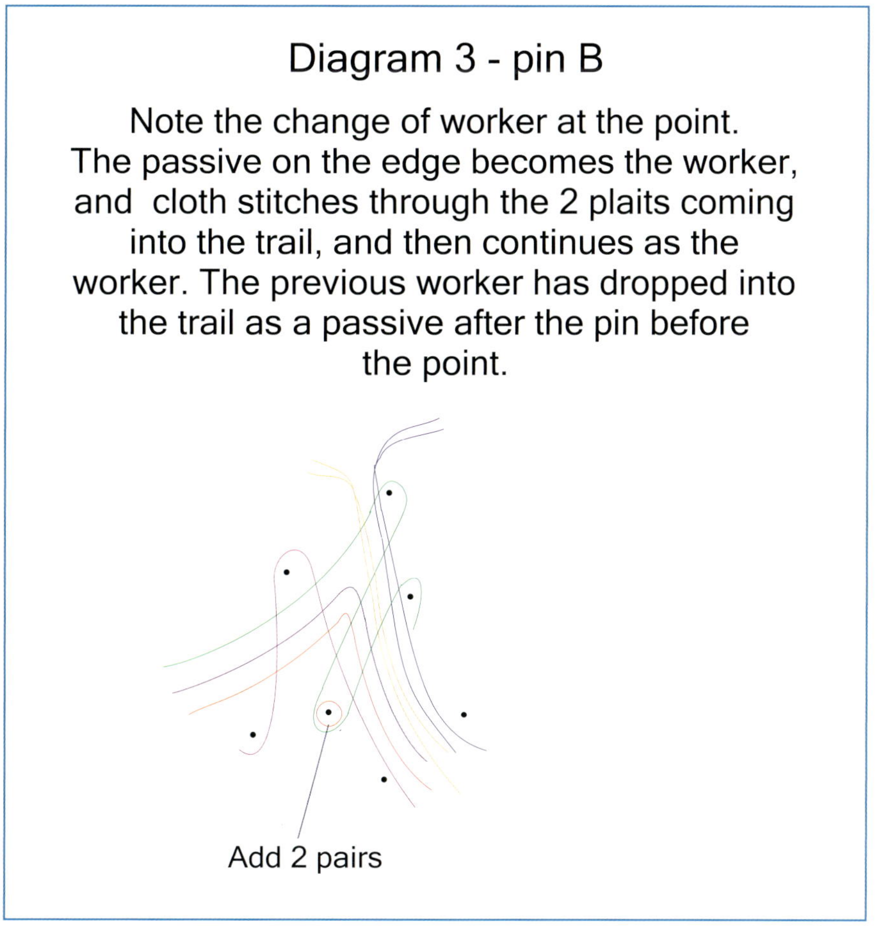

The central horizontal leaf tallies work from the left to the right, joining the trail at pin C. The leaf tally pairs are taken in on the left of the trail, and two pairs left out on the right at this pin.

Diagram 4

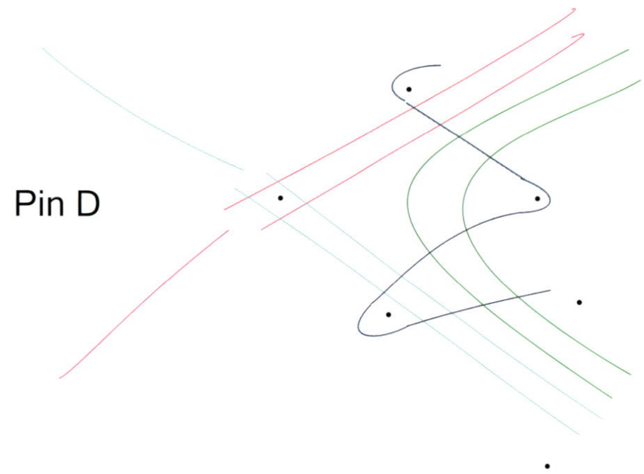

The plaits entering the trail at pin D cloth stitch through the first 2 passives, and these 2 passives become the plait leaving the trail. Note the pin is covered by the last cloth stitch

Pin D is worked by taking the pairs from the leaf tally in, and leaving two pairs out for each plait, using the pin on the inside edge twice.

Pin E is worked by taking pairs from the leaf in on the inside and leaving pairs out for plaits, using the inside pin twice.

Pin F is the finishing pin for the two trails to join at. Pairs are reduced just before this pin is worked.

Diagram 5

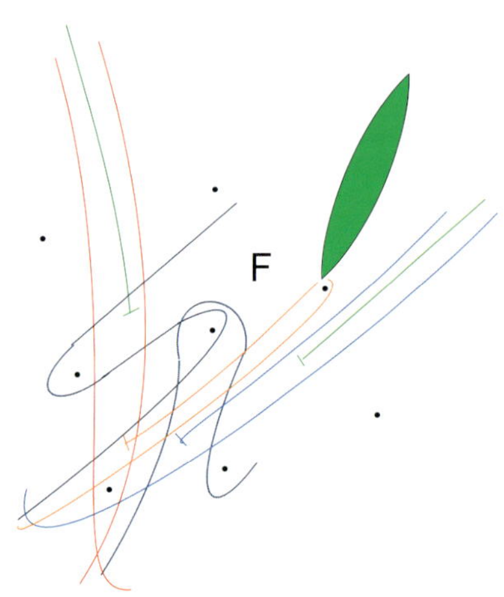

The 2 trails meet at pin F.
Pairs are reduced by throwing out until 2 passives and a worker remain on each side.
Workers cloth stitch together at last inside pin and cloth stitch back through to outside edge.
Pairs on left trail cloth stitch through right trail pairs, ending with 2 plaits, each having 3 pairs in them.

7

Hexagonal Mat

The pattern has a traditional nine pin edge, making it one of the few patterns in the book that has retained this traditional edge. Many lacemakers prefer to use an alternative to this, but the half stitch oval shape in the edge adds interest by breaking up the nine pin and so retained for this pattern.

Made in Presencia Finca 60, uses 34 pairs.

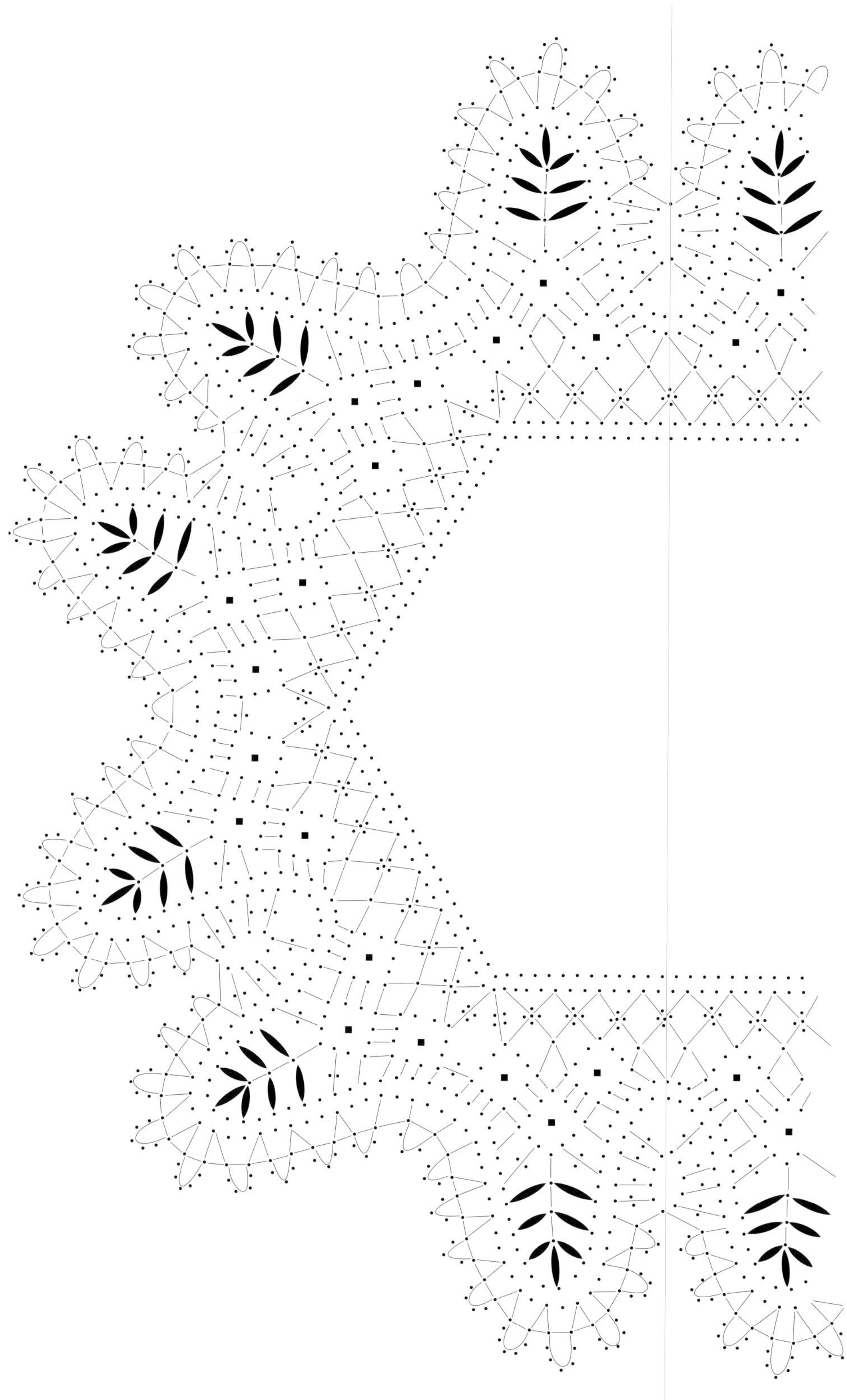

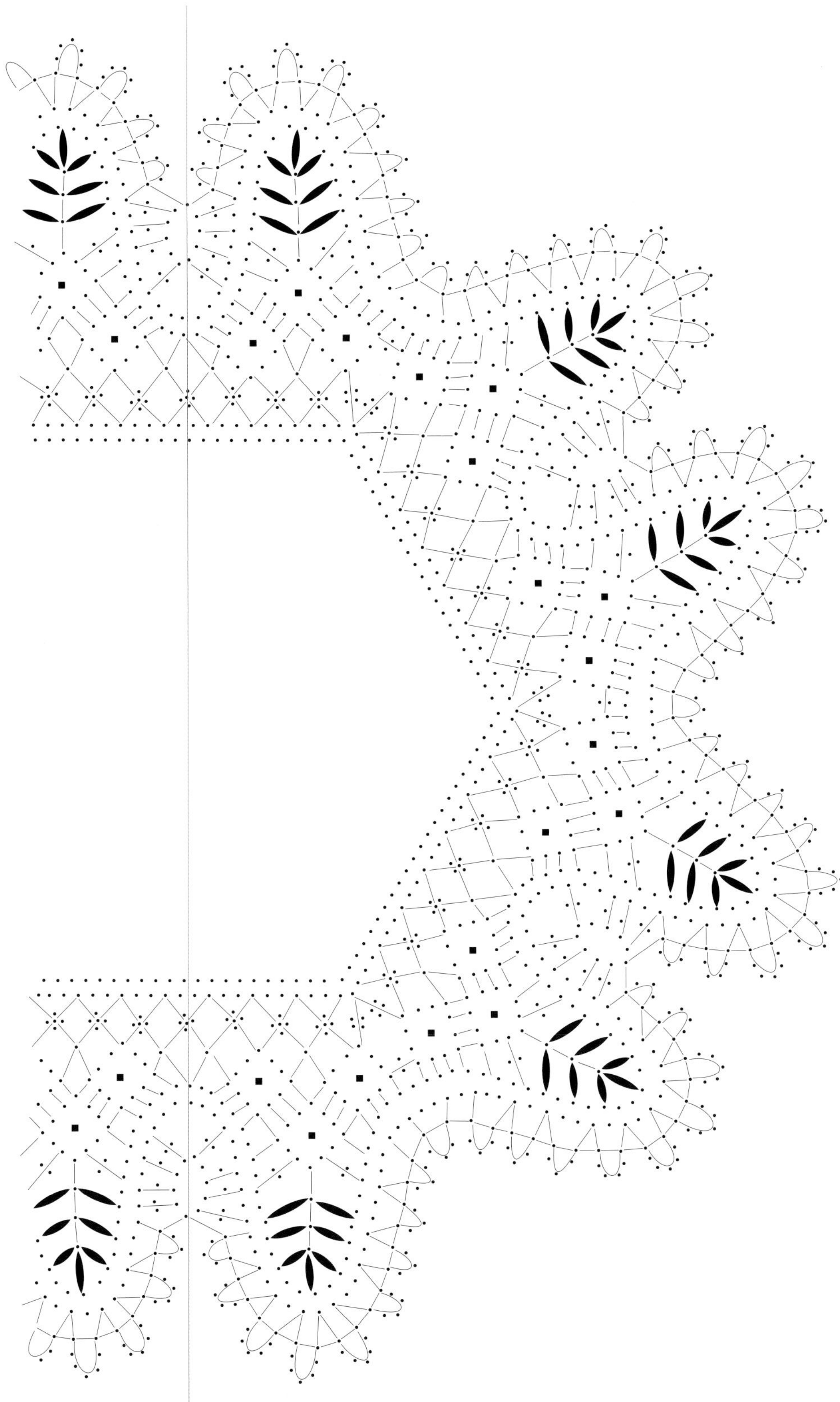

The headside edge trail requires five pairs to be put in and thrown out on each repeat. The design uses twisted pairs in place of plaits on the diamonds to reduce the quantity of pairs needed. These are adequate in this situation, as there is a twisted pair from each pin on the side of the diamond. On the opposite side, where there are only two lines indicates a plait rather than a twisted pair.

This pattern includes raised and rolled tallies over the half stitch diamonds.

Bedfordshire lace is traditionally worked from the front (i.e. not turned over when completed) to allow the working of any raised elements to the front of the lace.

Blossom filling

This version of Blossom filling is the Bedfordshire version. Anyone used to the Honiton version should take note that the Bedfordshire version is worked slightly differently. It has five holes where the Honiton version has four.

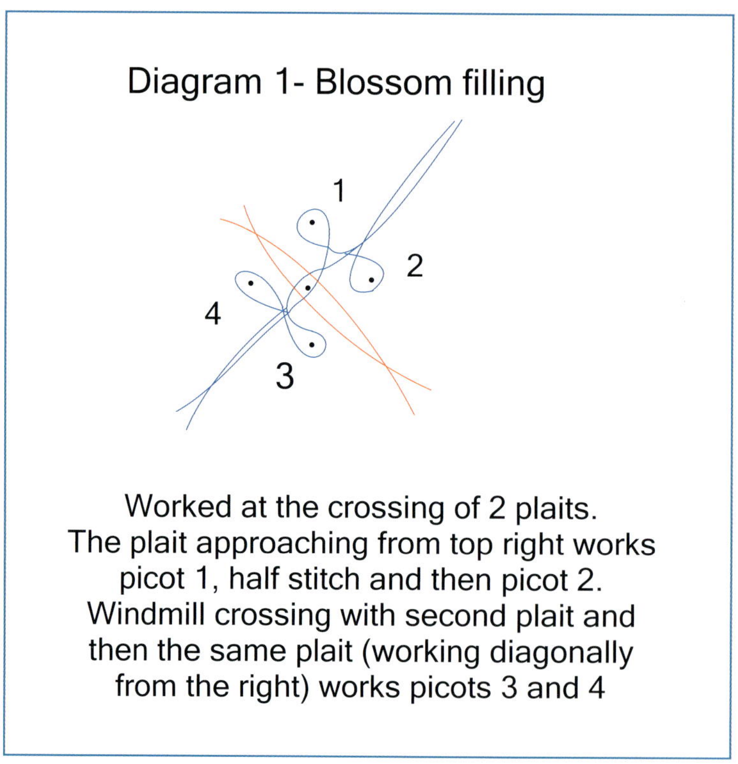

8

FLORAL EGG

Made in Presencia Finca 60 with approximately 90 pairs.

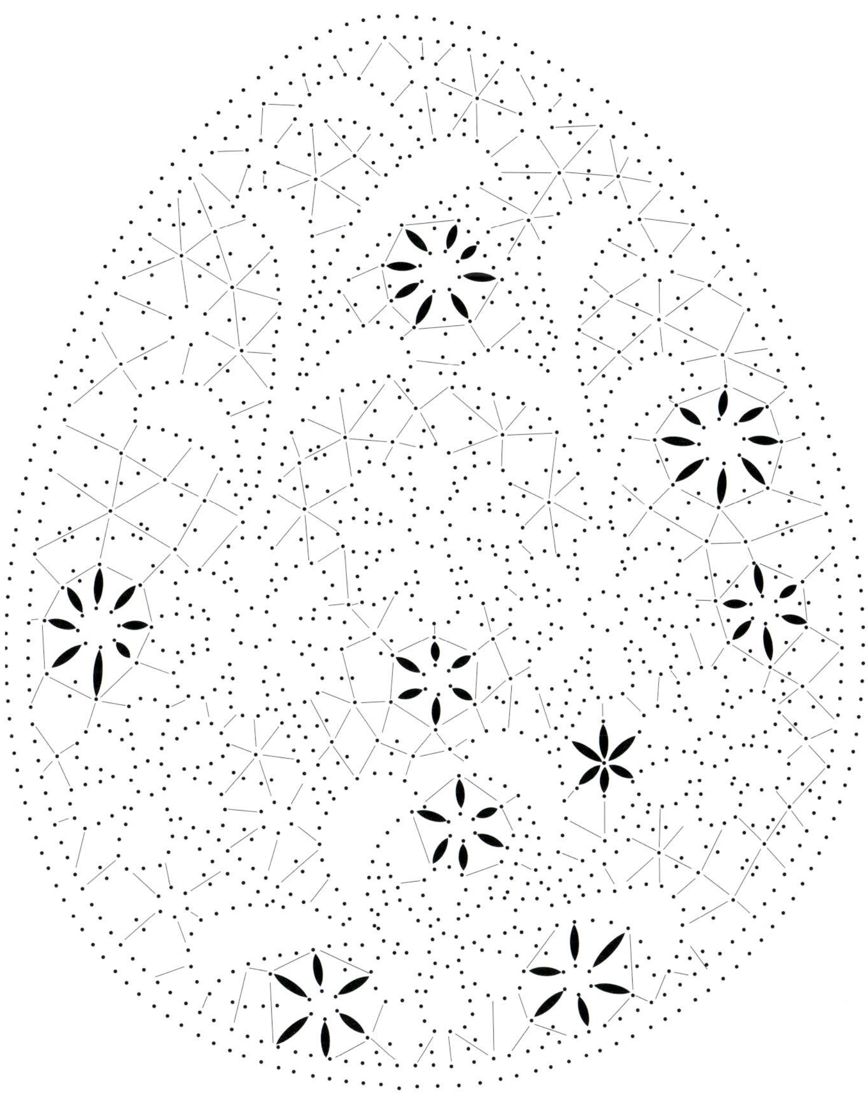

The patterns are now becoming more advanced. More pairs of bobbins need adding and throwing out throughout the piece.

Less detailed instructions will now be given, as more decisions are taken individually by the lacemaker. From now on you will have much greater opportunity to interpret the designs based on your individual experience and preferences.

The outer trail is started using a false picot. Pairs are then laid in both directions, with the pairs from the picot becoming the workers for each direction.

For the false picot, hang two pairs in open formation over the pin, put five twists on one of the pairs and then cloth stitch the two pairs together. The pairs are then ready to work through passives.

The only other technique not yet

encountered in this book is the start of the leaves at the top of this motif. There are several pin holes in a horizontal line. These pins have two pairs hung on each of them, and a pair works across the whole row to give a flat top to the leaf.

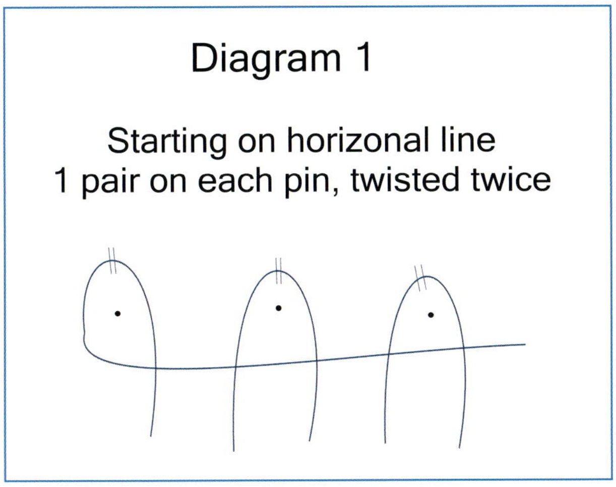

Throughout this pattern, pairs will need adding and throwing out to fill cloth stitch areas. The aim is to maintain the cloth stitch density, both filling the space between the pins and yet not packing it so much that it buckles and creates ripples in the work. It is a fine balance, but it gives the work a finesse that cannot be achieved without this attention to detail. Practice is needed to achieve the balance. To make the cloth stitch pleasing, you may have to undo your work to get the correct number of pairs in. Do not become disheartened if you have to rework it to achieve this. Even experienced lacemakers sometimes have this problem when tackling a new design.

Finishing an area of cloth on a horizontal line.

Diagram 2

Finishing a cloth stitch area on a horizontal line

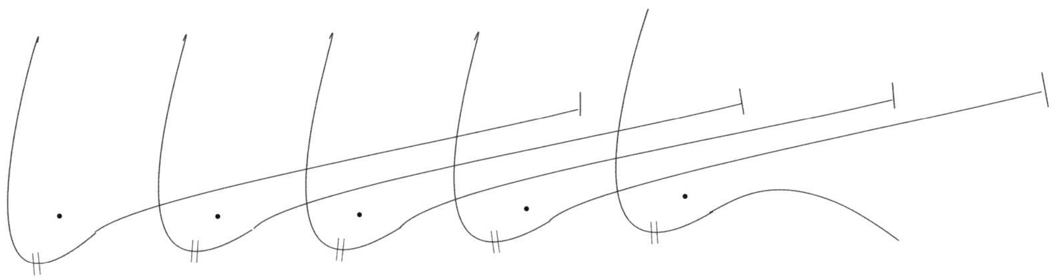

Each passive is worked - 2 twists, pin and then cloth stitched through a minimum of 3 pairs, before being thrown out.
Next passive repeats until the horizontal line is complete.
The last passive to be worked in this manner can become the worker to complete a stalk of the leaf, or go into a plait or leaf tally.
This reduces pairs quickly at the end of the cloth stitch area where a straight horizontal line finish is required.

9

DAISY BOOKMARK

Made in Presencia Finca 60, approximately 60+ pairs, but many are put in and then thrown out at the end of cloth stitch areas and so can be reused.

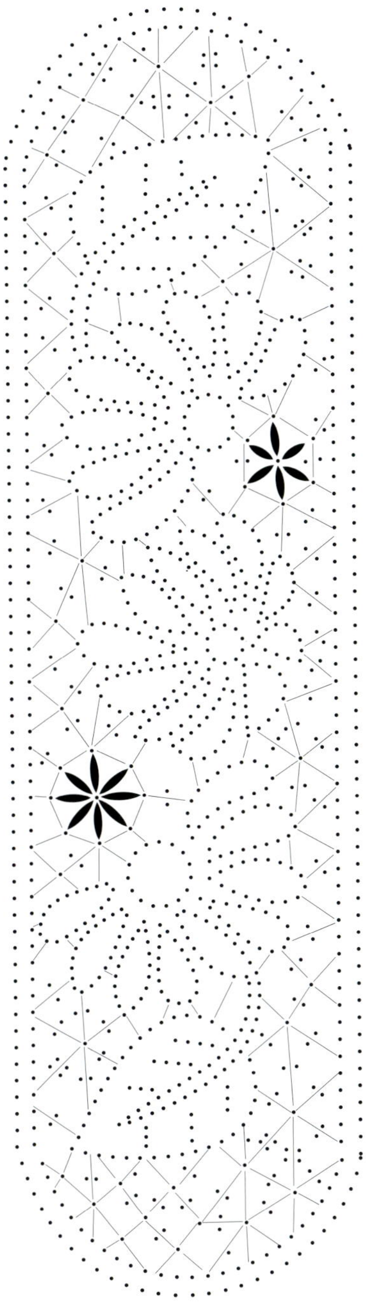

This pattern is the one of a series of designs that evolved incorporating the daisy motif. The first pattern designed was the handkerchief edging that follows, but the bookmark has been placed ahead of that, as it is smaller and easier to work. This will give you a taste of the design before you commit to a bigger project. It also incorporates the leaves with horizontal and vertical veins found in many traditional patterns.

The first leaf has a start on a horizontal line, as in the last pattern, although it requires more pairs across the row. The flowers are also smaller on this design than the handkerchief edging, and therefore fewer pairs are required to work it. However, every petal and leaf needs a number of bobbins adding and then throwing out on each element, a feature of floral designs. All the petals have a plait from the end that goes into the middle circle. This has not been marked on the pattern due to the small space between the two elements.

The bookmark can be finished off with a tassel in the centre or, as is shown in the photograph, slightly off centre without a tassel.

10

Daisy edging

Made in Presencia Finca 60. Approximately 70+ pairs which are used and thrown out regularly through the flowers.

Many lacemakers struggle to get to grips with starting a piece of lace. The main thing to consider is not where to start, but where you want to finish the piece, particularly when working edgings. On finishing a piece of lace, the main aim is to join the end to the start while making it as invisible as possible. This is achieved most successfully if you join into cloth stitch areas. Also, you can deceive the viewer's eye and more effectively hide the join if you zig-zag across the design, rather than working a straight line. If you are working a motif, try not to finish at the central point as it will be much more obvious than if the join it slightly off centre. The early patterns in this book show the starting point to help you with this and invariably start on cloth stitch areas.

Of all the patterns in this book, this is the oldest. It is printed as it was designed and worked. Although now with more design experience, if it were designed today it would probably include picots on many of the plaits, particularly between the headside and the daisies. You can make the decision whether to add these and improve the design by adding them to the longer plaits and windmill crossings, as was the case in the previous bookmark plaits, or you can simply follow the design and work the pattern without.

The pattern has an alternative nine pin edge, which adds variety by having the leaf tallies on alternate heads. This adds weight to the design to balance the heavy areas of cloth stitch.

This pattern also has overlaid leaf tallies on top of the half stitch in the centre of the daisies, giving a three dimensional element to the flowers. There are also raised and rolled tallies on the half stitch buds at the corners.

All the petals have a plait from the end that goes into the middle circle. This has not been marked on the pattern due to the small space between the two elements.

11

DAISY OVAL MOTIF

Made in Presencia Finca 60, approximately 70+ pairs.

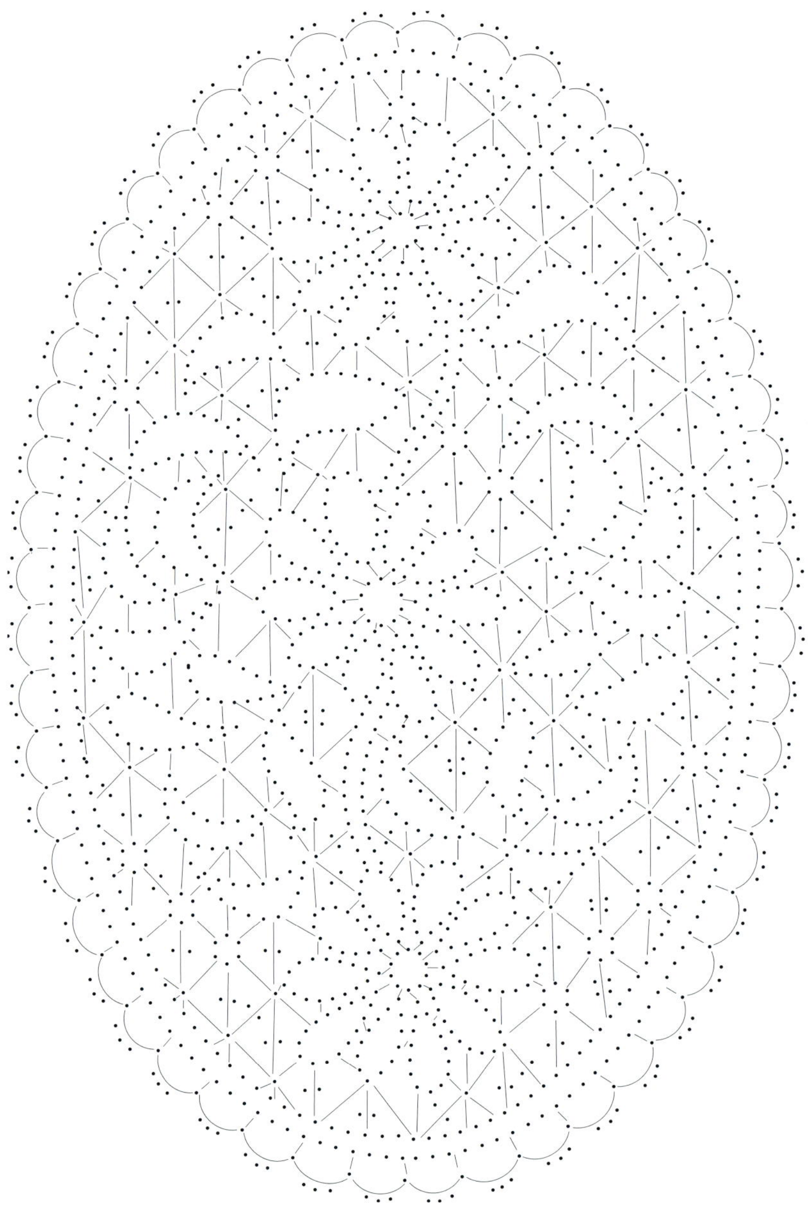

This design repeats the motif used in the previous two patterns, but with a variation: The centre of the flowers is not worked in half stitch as previously, but by cloth stitching the pairs through each other.

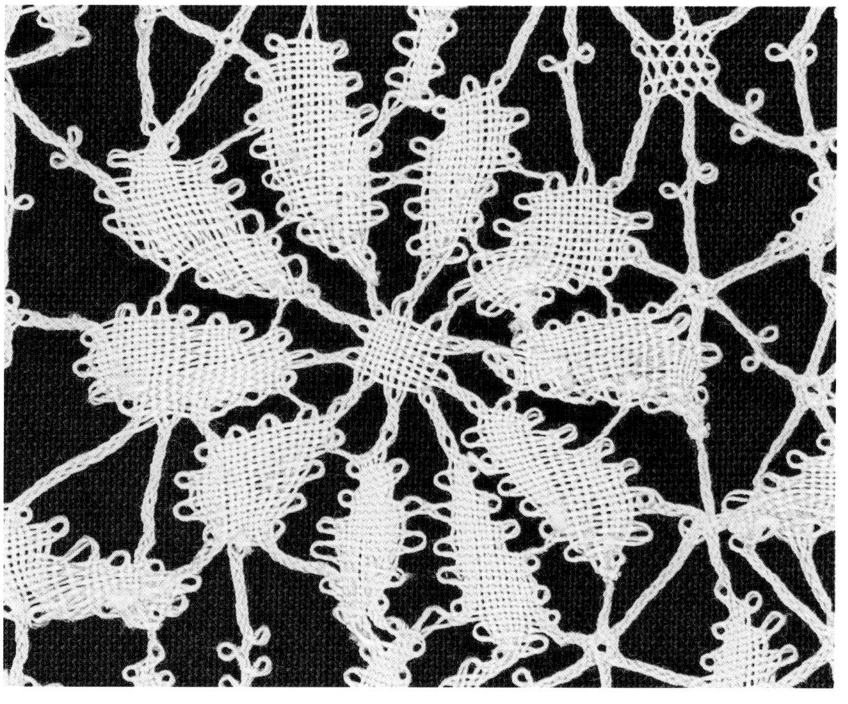

Close up of flower centre

This technique is seen on antique lace and would have been much quicker to work than using half stitch in this situation. Pins are placed at the ends of each plait, and then the four pairs from the left, cloth stitch through the four pairs from the right, before putting the pins in between pairs to start the plaits which start each new petal. Alternatively half stitch buds can be used.

Antique lace showing this technique

Many lacemakers find it tedious to use nine pin edging in Bedfordshire. This pattern uses an alternative to the traditional one found on pattern 7, with other variations found on patterns 10, 12 and 19. This variation uses cucumber tallies that are made with the workers from the trail and the inside pair from the plait. The tally should be wider than it is long.

12

LEAF MOTIF

Made in Presencia Finca 60, approximately 60 pairs.

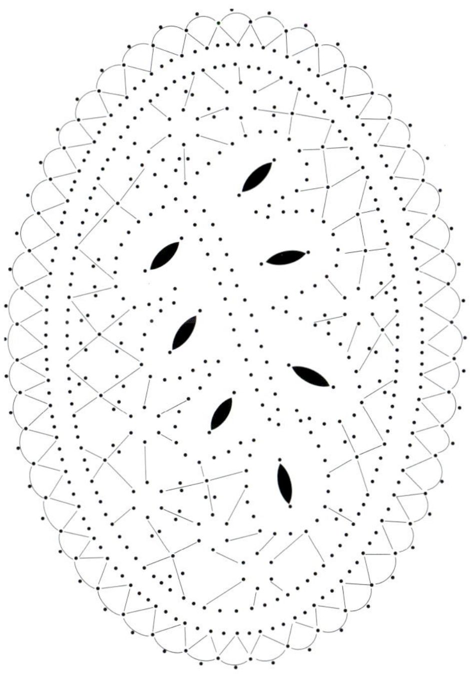

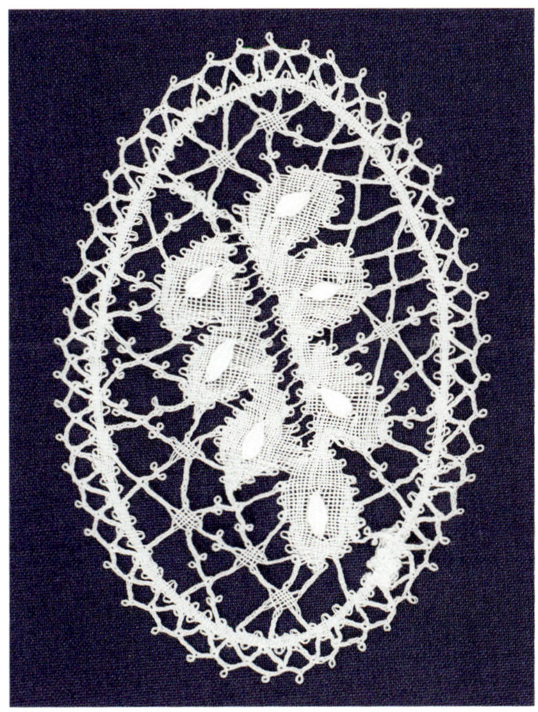

This small design features a traditional leaf found in many antique patterns. It is found in many of the Harry Armstrong designs of the Bucks Cottage Workers Association from around 1910. It is a smaller version of the leaf in the pattern that follows. It is worked in cloth stitch and has overlaid leaf tallies. The design also includes the 'spots' between the plaits which can be worked as half stitch. They are worked here with cloth stitch, as discussed in the previous pattern. This design is intended to give you a small motif to work, enabling you to try the leaf without committing to a larger piece of lace. It has a simple edging of two interlocking plaits. Most designs need something on the edge to make it look complete, but this is a simple alternative when a plainer edge look is required.

It is always useful to work a small motif to try out part of designs that you are not familiar with. Finished motifs make for nice gifts for anyone who appreciates handmade presents.

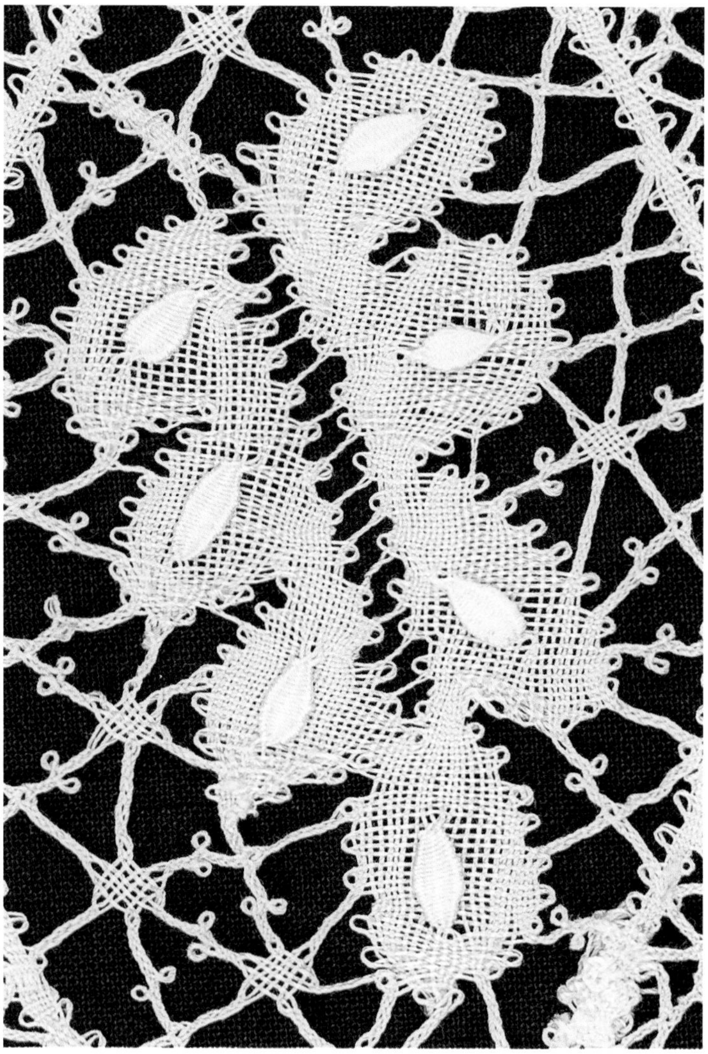

Part of an antique collar showing the use of this leaf, in collection of the author.

Close up of antique lace showing gimped veins.

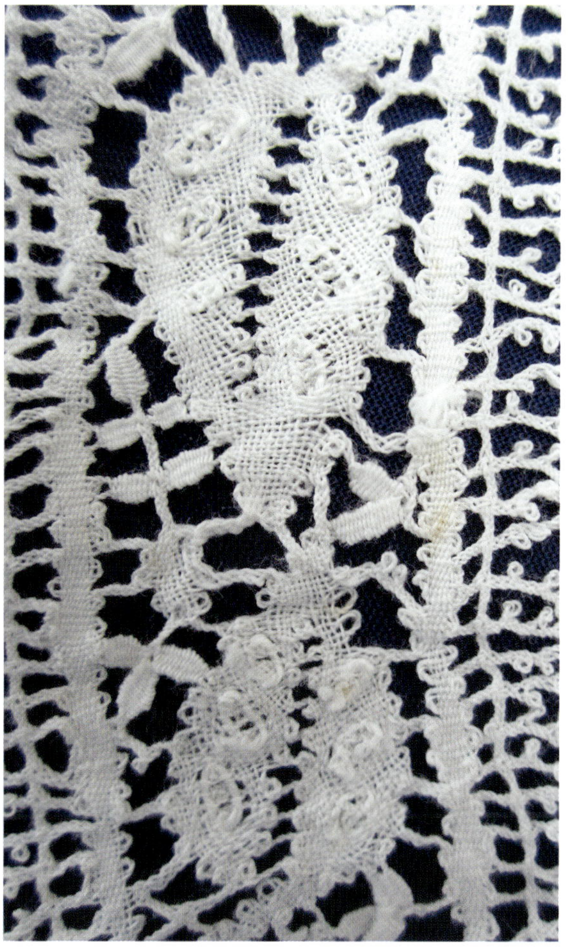

Over the years there has been much discussion over the use of gimps in Bedfordshire lace. Many pieces can be worked successfully with or without gimps, and the use of them is very often down to the individual lacemaker's preference. For a gimp to be used today, it needs to add something to the design. This can be emphasising a feature within the design, or to make it appear more three dimensional. But it needs to have a function, and not just added for the sake of it. In many antique pieces the gimp adds nothing to the character of the lace. It has clearly been used simply as a quick means of filling the space. The thick thread filled up an area, making it much quicker to work, and therefore more economic when the lacemakers were competing against the machines taking over their trade. Today lacemakers are not generally being paid for their work. They are doing it for pleasure, and are thus free to strive for a perfection that would not have been possible in the 19th century. So use gimps if you wish, but first consider their use, and ask yourself whether they add anything to the design. For instance, gimps can look messy if they are only used to outline one or two pinholes on a vein.

13

ASYMMETRIC DAISY MOTIF

Made in Presencia Finca 60, approximately 70 pairs.

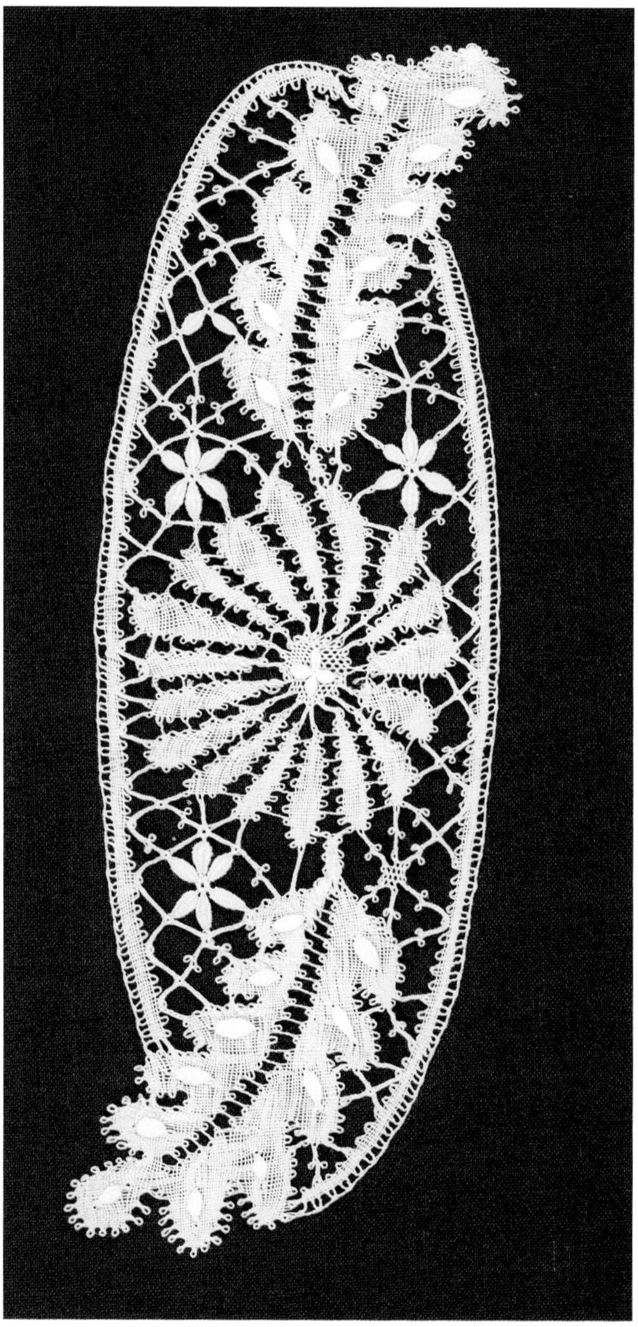

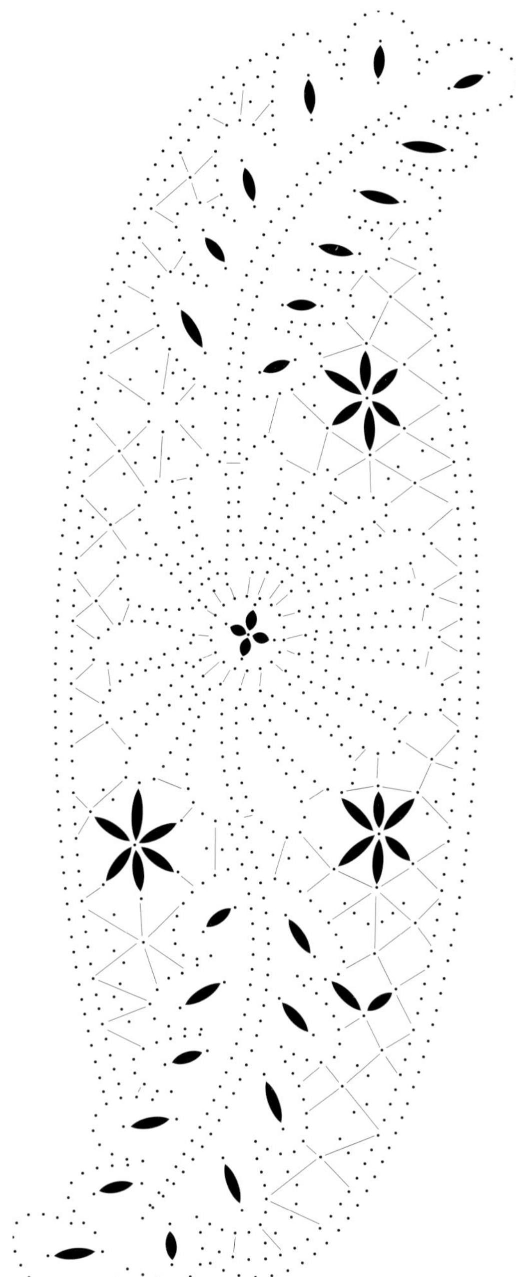

With the flow of the leaves throughout the flower, this pattern has a feel of movement. It incorporates a larger version of the leaves from the previous pattern with one of the daisies that originated on the handkerchief edging. It also has the challenge of finishing at the bottom of the leaf on the edge. But as the leaf reduces and pairs are thrown out, there are actually only a handful of pairs to be fastened off.

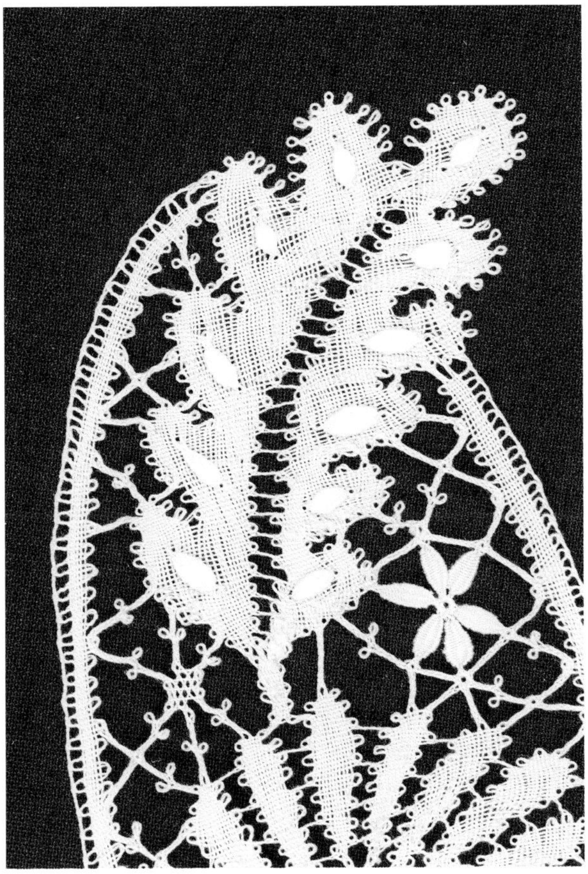

The leaf part that is growing beyond the oval frame has picots on the outside, but any pin holes on the inside of this frame are worked without. The outline trail is worked with a change of worker edge to give a clean and crisp frame.

14

DAISY AND LEAF BOOKMARK

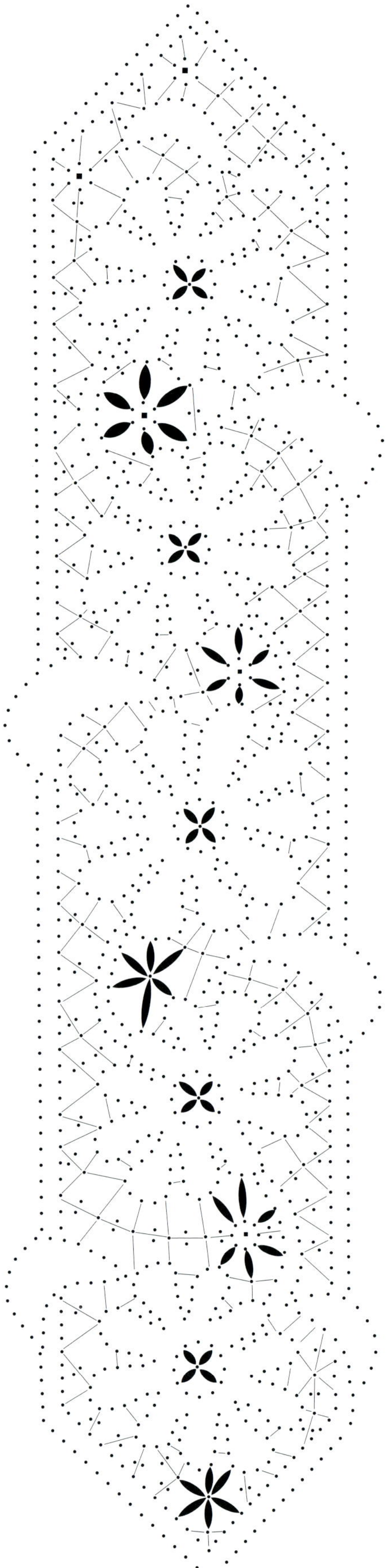

Made in Presencia Finca 60, approximately 50 pairs.

This pattern has a slightly different variety of daisy as the main flower. The petals are all joined and the centre is open with leaf tallies across it. The outside leaves break through the edges of the bookmark as if growing beyond it.

There are also raised and rolled tallies on the half stitch buds.

15

Fantasy flowers motif

Made in Presencia Finca 60, approximately 80 pairs.

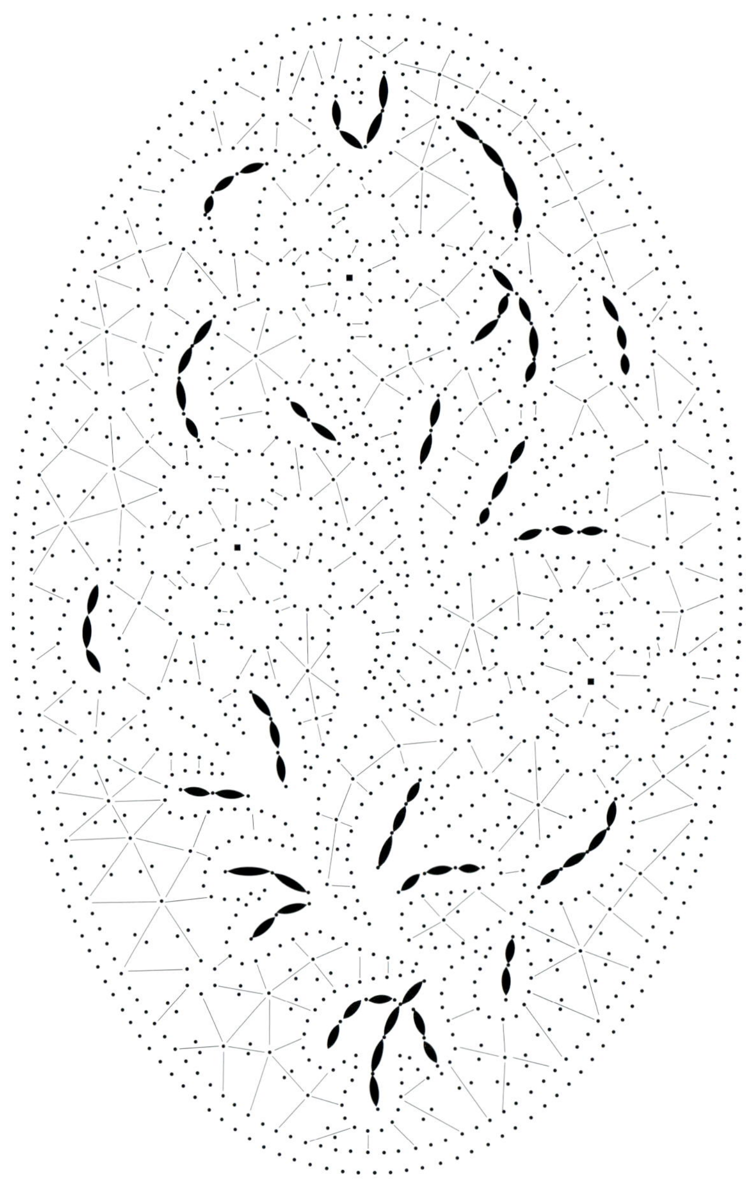

This motif incorporates round globe-like flowers of half stitch with overlaid leaf tallies in place of veins, and raised and rolled tallies on the flower centres. The flower is reminiscent of the drumstick primula (Primula denticulata), although both the flower and leaves are stylised. Hence the pattern's name "Fantasy flowers".

Diagonal veins can look untidy when worked in leaves. This pattern explores an alternative, using overlaid leaf tallies to give the impression of a raised central vein on the plant leaf.

One of the main characteristics of Bedfordshire lace is the use and inclusion of flowers and plants within the designs. Bedfordshire lace developed during the second half of the 19th century, when plant hunters were bringing back such exotic plants that the Victorians had not seen before. The Victorians had a particular fascination with exotic plants, and these featured in the fashions of the time. Some of the flowers included in the designs are recognisable as flowers. Others are less distinct, and towards the end of the century they were becoming increasingly less defined. Flowers and leaves still form the basis of many designs today, acting as the focal point in the designs.

Example of a stylised flower in an antique piece of lace, in the collection of the author.

This example shows a flower among a spray of leaves. It has been so stylised from the original inspiration that it has become an unrecognisable flower. It also shows the use of gimps around veins, sometimes only two pins.

Four flowers in Bedfordshire lace, different styles and centres.

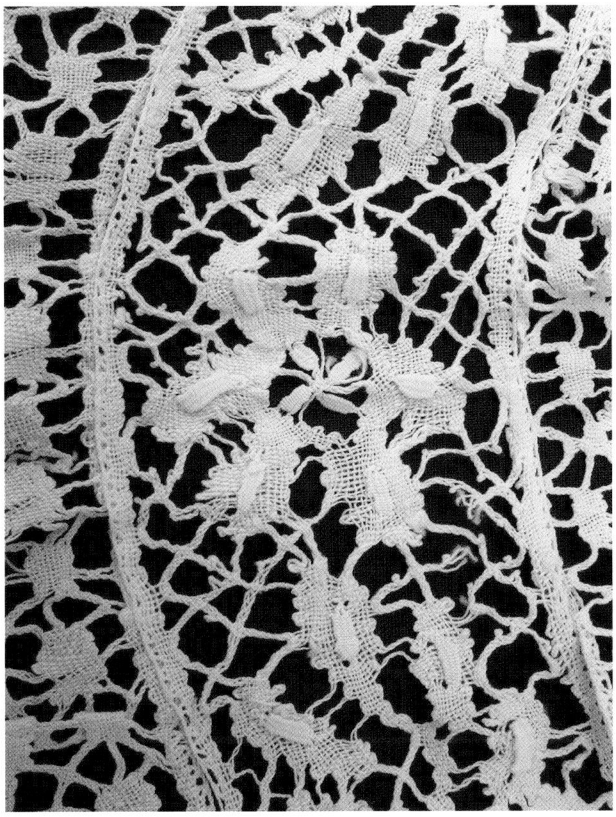

All four are antique lace.

16

Heart Motif

Made in Presencia Finca 60 thread, approximately 60+ pairs.

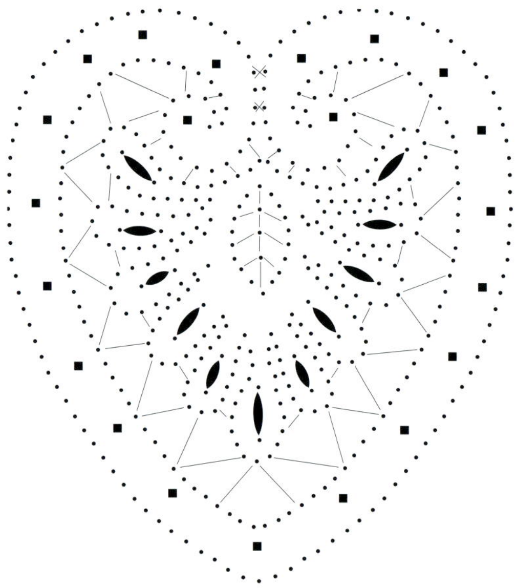 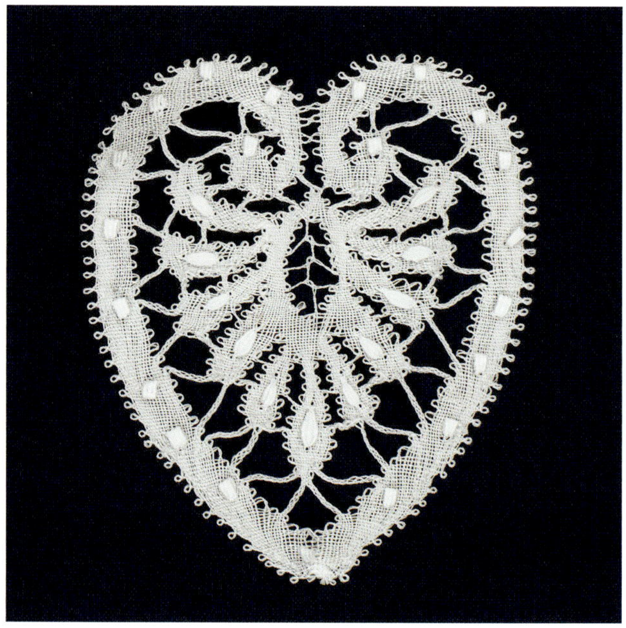

A small but perfectly formed heart. It looks deceptively small, but a quantity of bobbins is required for the piece, with numerous pairs being put in for the cloth stitch and then thrown out again. The leaf in the centre has overlaid leaf tallies, and the heart edging has raised and rolled tallies. The biggest challenge with this piece is keeping the cloth stitch a consistent density while also leaving out pairs for the overlaid elements.

The piece is started with a number of false picots on a horizontal line.

Note the central vein has been worked using twisted pairs instead of plaits. This gives space to another otherwise solid cloth stitch area.

17

Silver Dollar Tulips

Made in Presencia Finca 60, approximately 80 pairs.

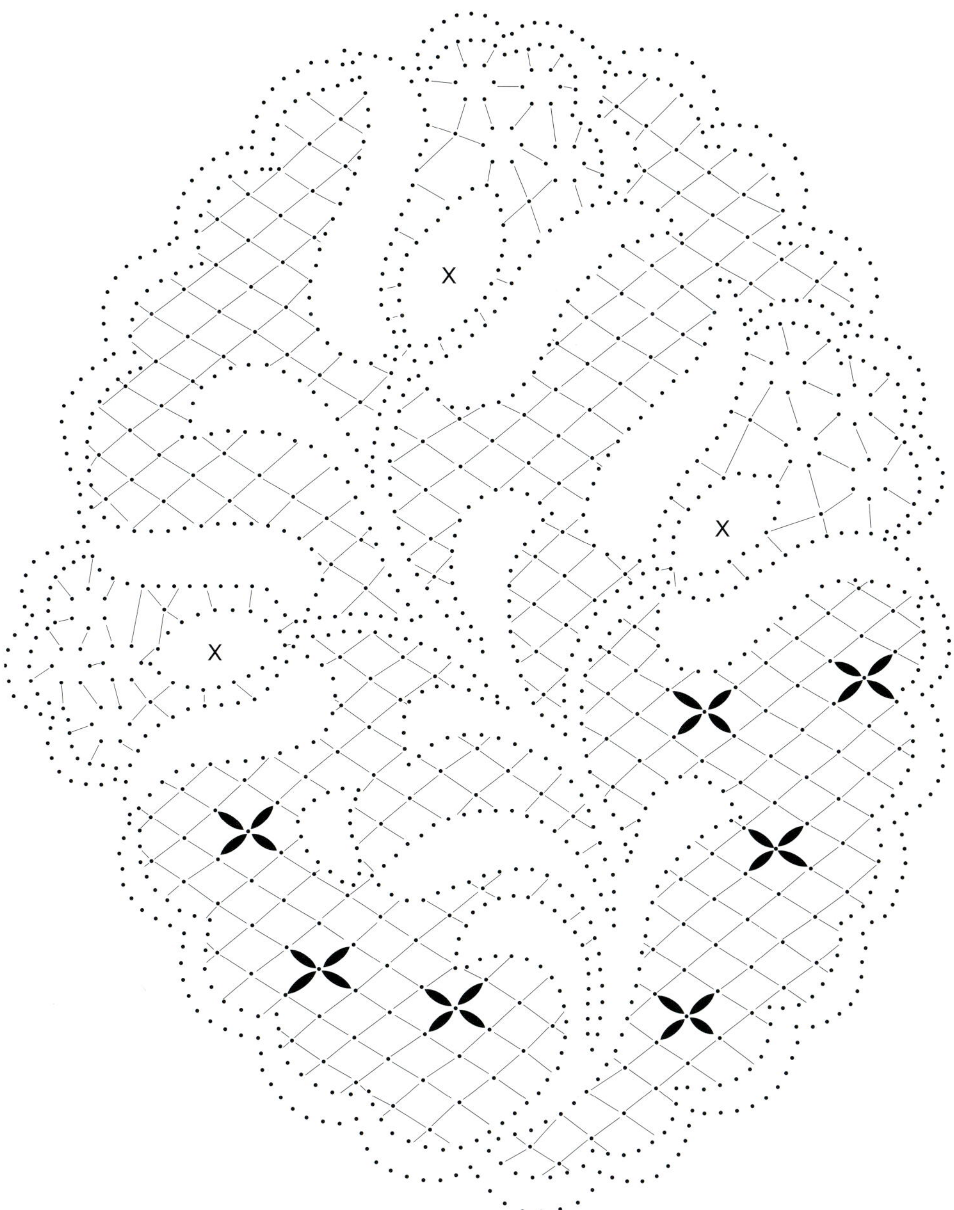

This pattern was designed and then worked for a competition, in which it came second. It was created to celebrate a silver anniversary and so a silver pair of workers were used on the edge trail. This is optional, and was just a personal choice made by the lacemaker. It also has the worker pairs twisted on each row of this edge trail to introduce space in the trail. The pattern is fairly self-explanatory for designs at this stage of the book. The central petals of the flowers are marked with 'X' to indicate that half stitch is used within this petal.

18

Spider Chrysanthemums

Made in Presencia Finca 60, approximately 110 pairs.

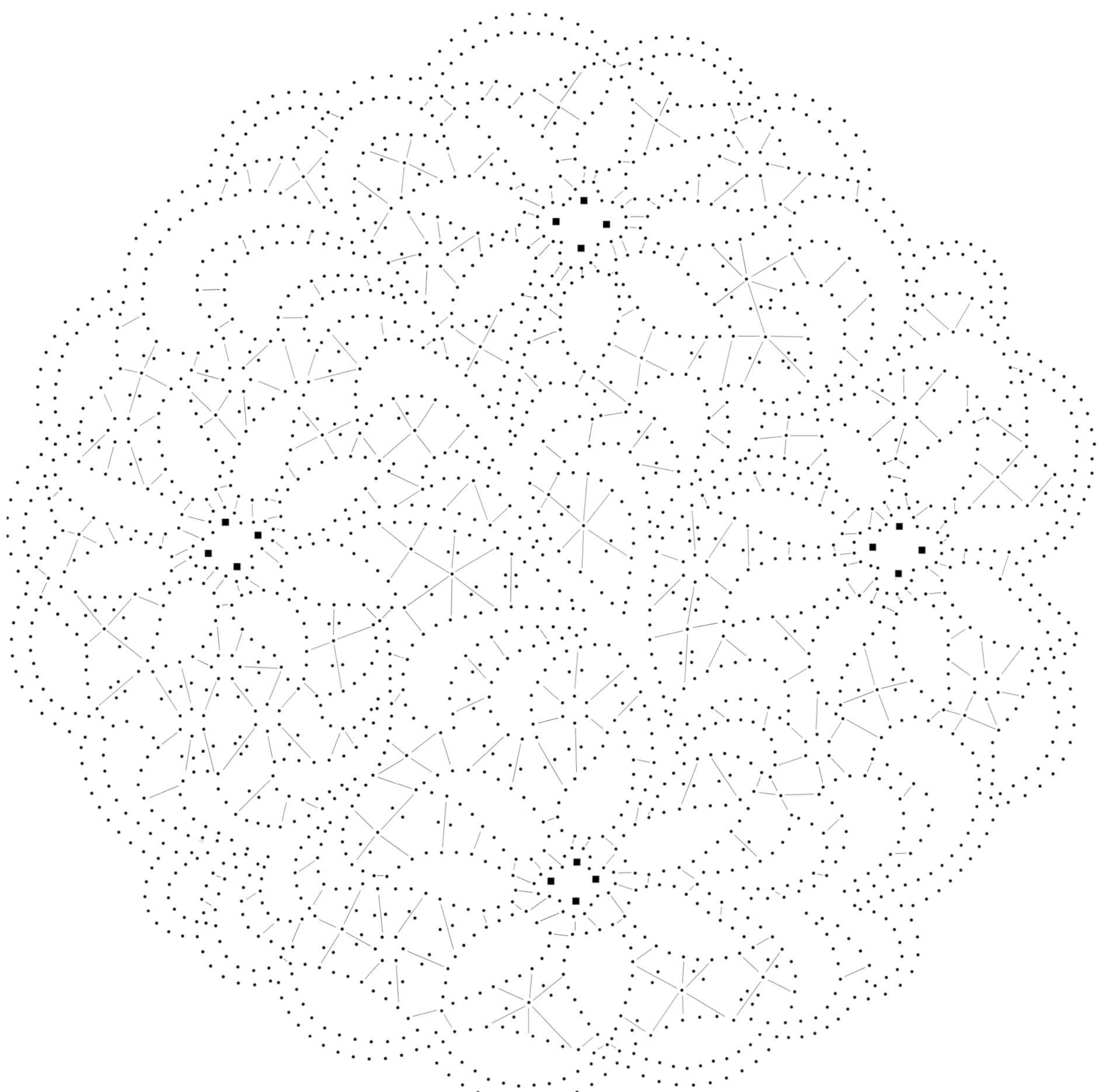

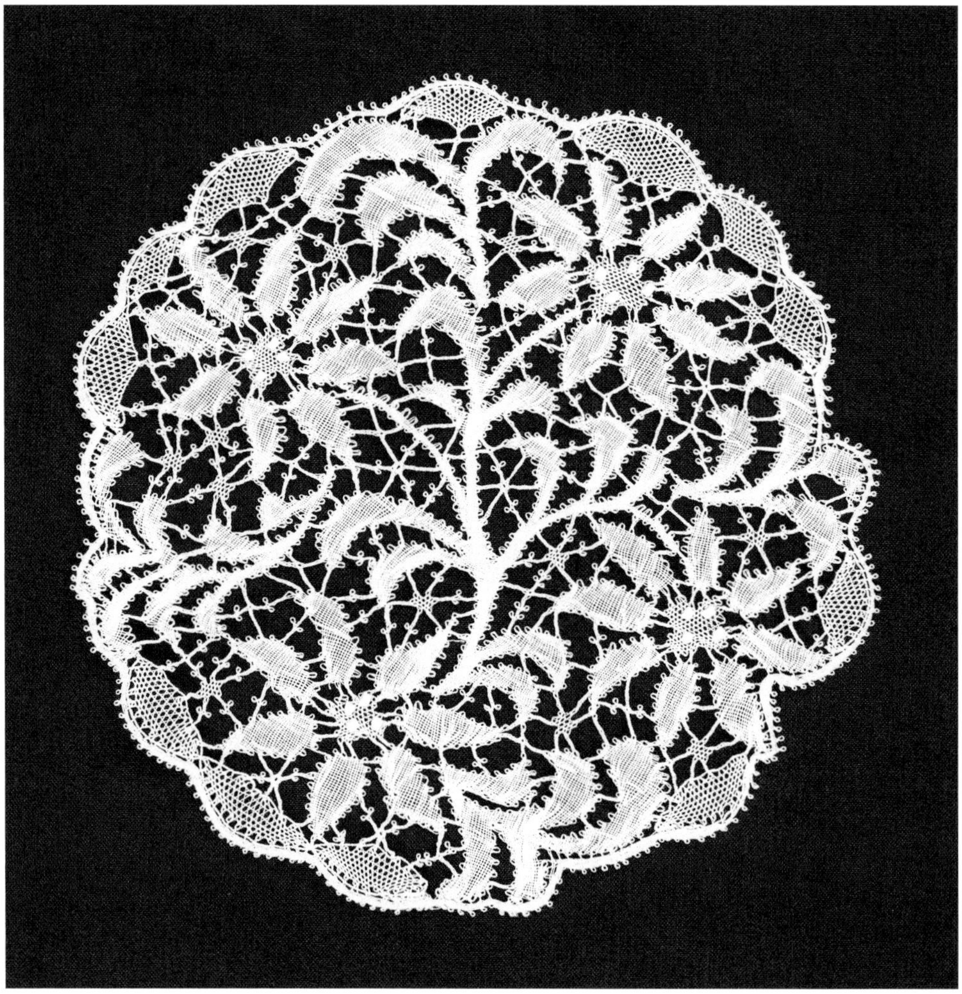

This design is one of very few in the book that has used a gimp to outline the half stitch on the edge of the motif. It was used to try and give a little more weight to the edge while retaining the airiness of the half stitch, balancing the weight of the large flowers.

19

Daisies and Fern

This pattern was designed to give a bigger mat that does not require mounting on to fabric on completion. It is an ideal pattern if you are looking for a larger and more interesting project, and it can be mounted under glass in a tray. It is worked around the design, in an anticlockwise direction, rather than top to bottom.

Made in Presencia Finca 60, approximately 130 pairs.

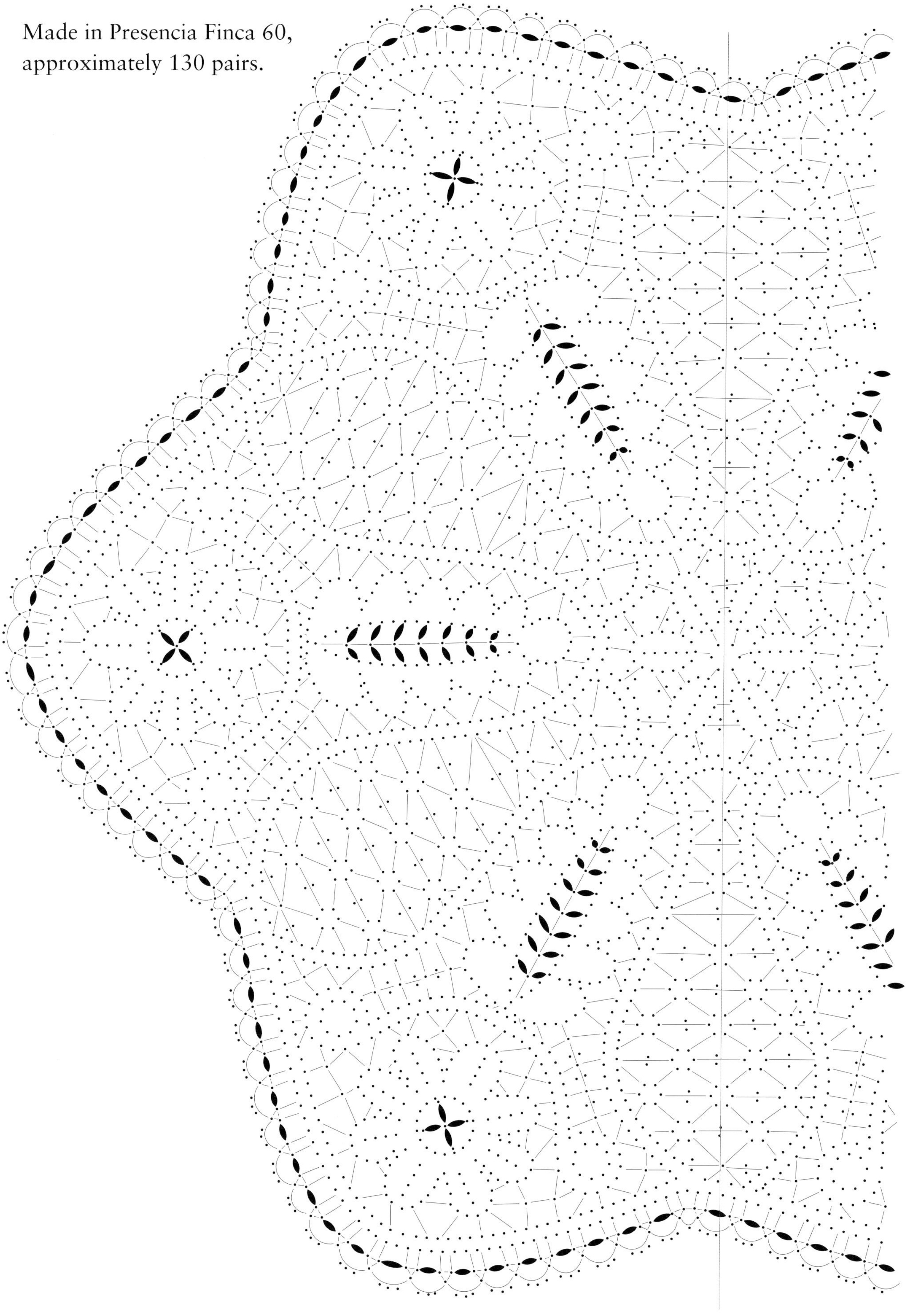

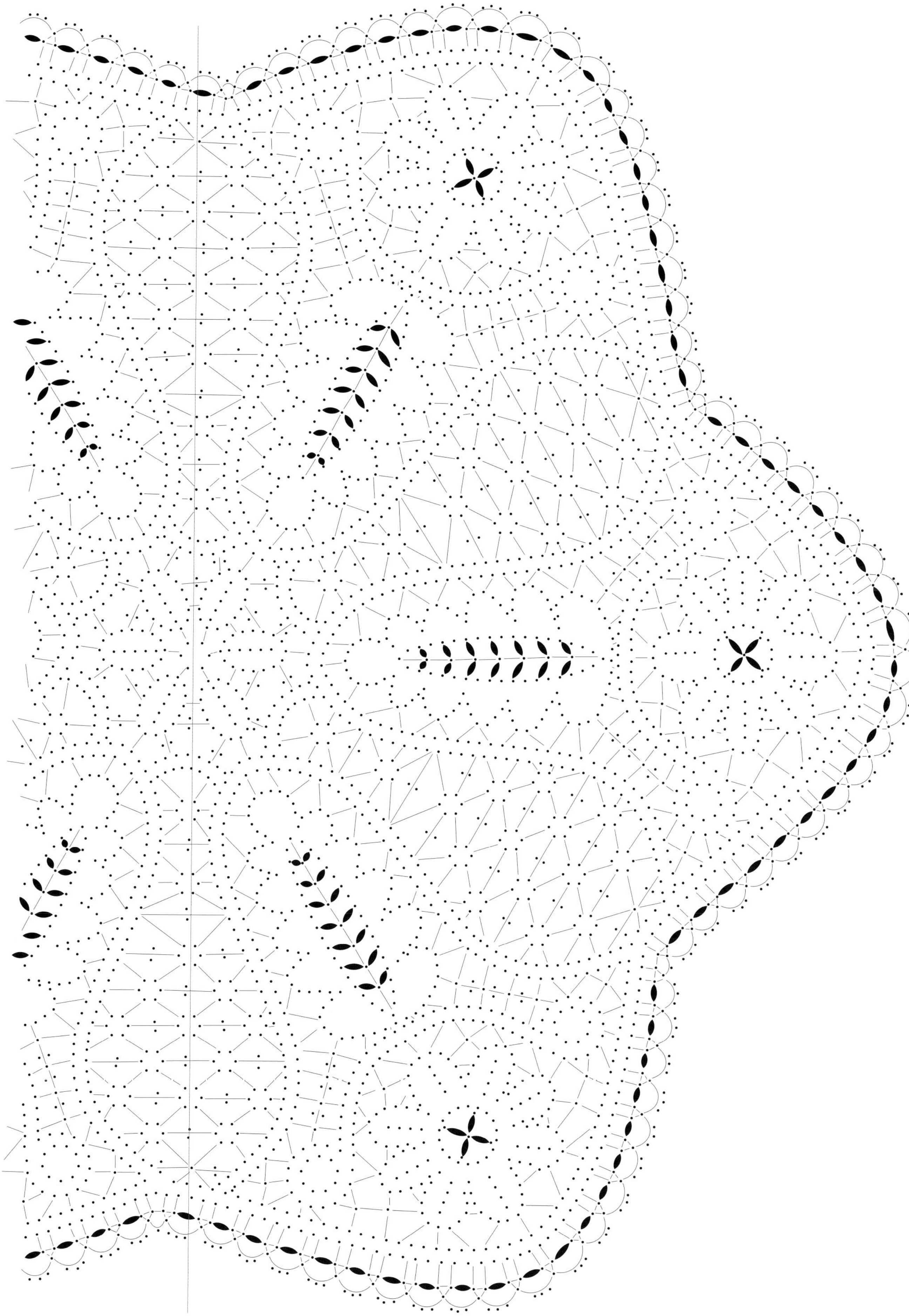

Close up showing detail of flower with vertical, horizontal and box veins, according to direction of the petal and leaf.

The design makes use of a popular edging that gives more weight to the design than the basic nine pin edging.

Similar flower in antique edging

Similar leaf in antique edging

20

Swirling Leaves

Made in Presencia Finca 60, approximately 60 pairs.

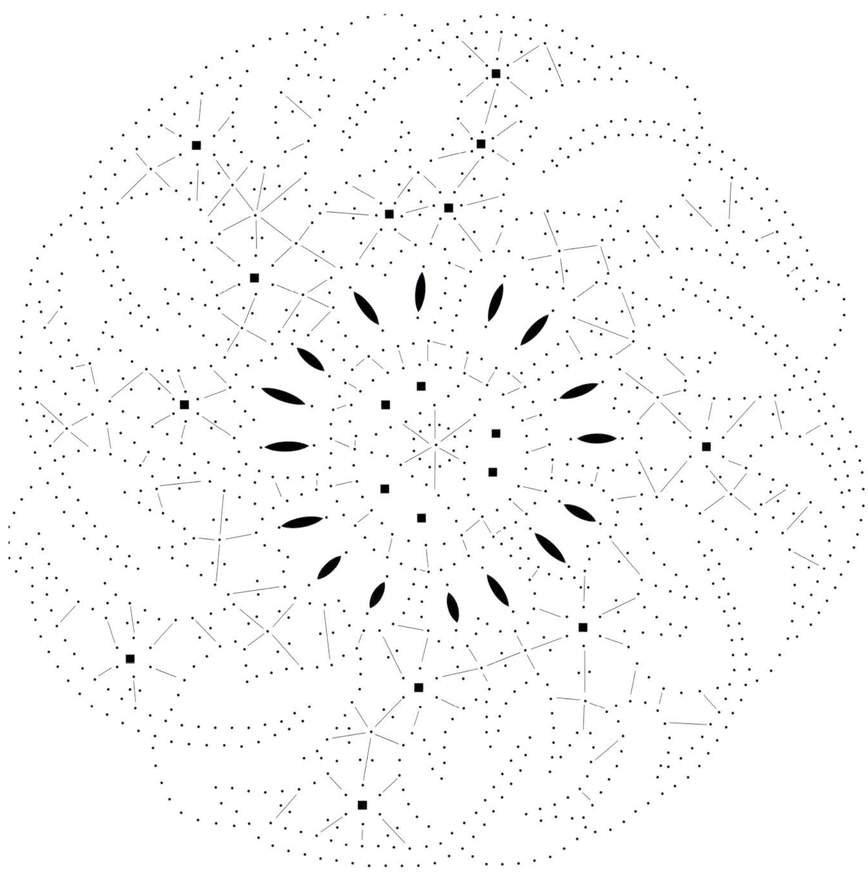

The pattern is worked around the design in an anticlockwise direction around the centre pin.

Note on the short edge of the cloth stitch area with the overlaid leaf tallies, the pin holes need to be used twice on this right hand side.

21

CARNATION

Made in Presencia Finca 60, approximately 80 pairs, with many pairs being put in and thrown out, particularly with all the cloth stitch circles in the design.

This pattern has the addition of raised and rolled tallies over the top of the windmill crossings. This technique was used regularly in the grounds of Thomas Lester designs in the 19th century. It adds a three dimensional element to the ground.

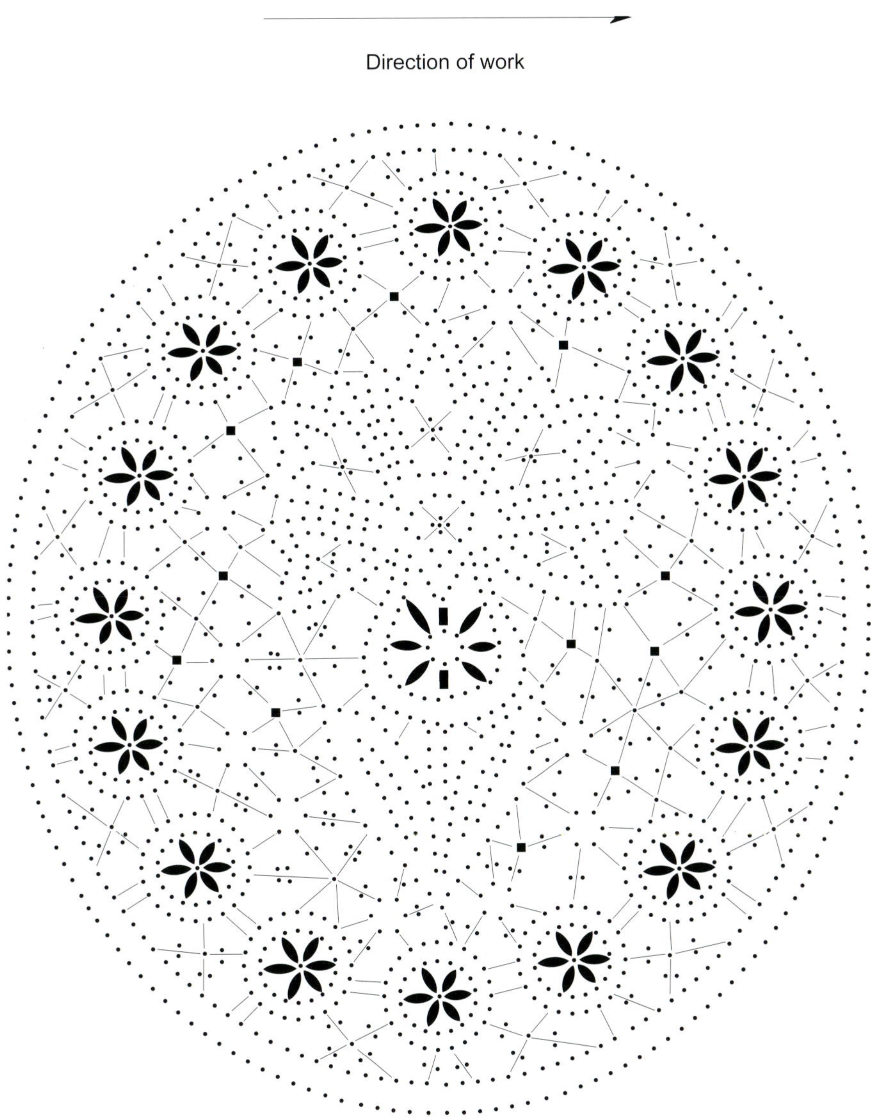

Raised and rolled tallies over the windmill crossing

The tally is worked after the first part of the windmill crossing. In effect, this is a half stitch using the four pairs as single bobbins. The pin is put in to hold the windmill crossing, and the raised and rolled tally is worked using the outside two pairs, pairs one and four. To roll the tally, the pin is removed and the tally rolled, with the pin being placed across the work, flat onto the pillow. The two pairs that worked the tally are placed in the original position on the outside of the other two pairs. This allows for the crossing to be completed and then the next plaits made.

The flower

Note the difference in marking on the pattern at the base of the carnation flower: six leaf shaped tallies plus two horizontally at the sides. These are worked as cucumber tallies, which appear to the eye to be the same, but it means that no extra pairs are needed to work them.

Working trail diagonally

This technique is for moving pairs across the trail in the direction the trail is travelling. The diagram shows the movement of pairs from the outside of the trail, across passives to the next pin on the inside edge, where it remains and drops down. It changes from a passive to a worker, and then back to a passive after the pin. This is the manner of working the diagonal trails used in this flower. One point to note is that in order to maintain the density of the cloth stitch, there needs to be enough pairs of passives in the trail prior to starting the movement. This is because only half the number of rows are worked and they are all worked in one direction, which reduces the density of the cloth stitch.

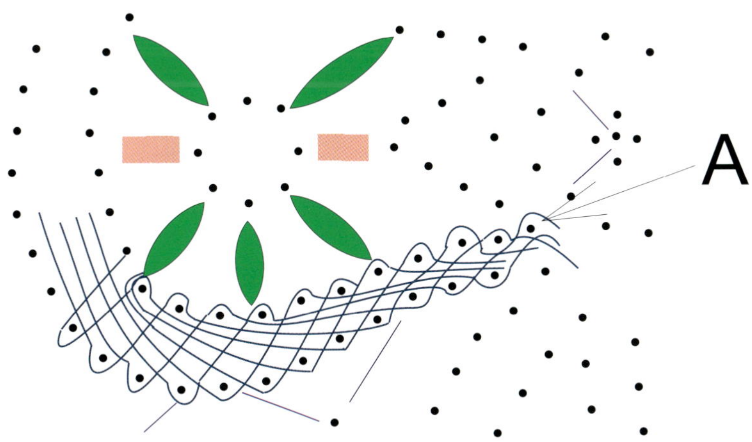

At pin A on the diagram, the pair that is travelling to this pin meets the worker from the adjoining trail in cloth stitch. Then one of the pairs becomes the worker for the combined trail, and the second pair becomes another passive. As there are a number of pairs joining from the left at this point, it is necessary to throw out pairs to ensure there are not too many pairs in the joined trail. It is therefore up to you to judge how many pairs to throw out.

22

Leafy oval motif

Made in Presencia Finca 80, approximately 90 pairs.

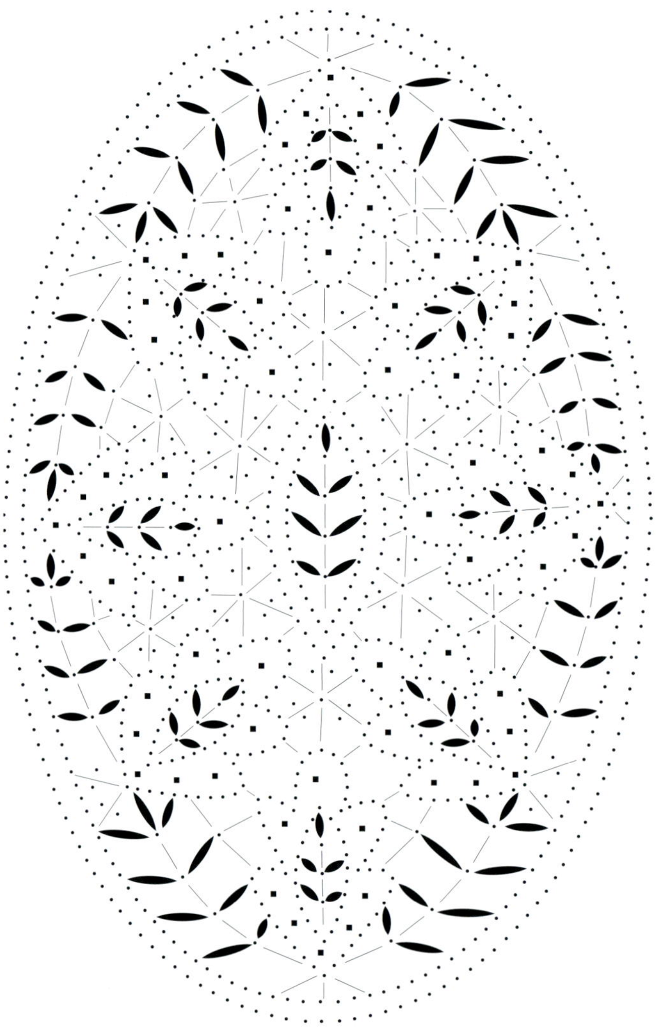

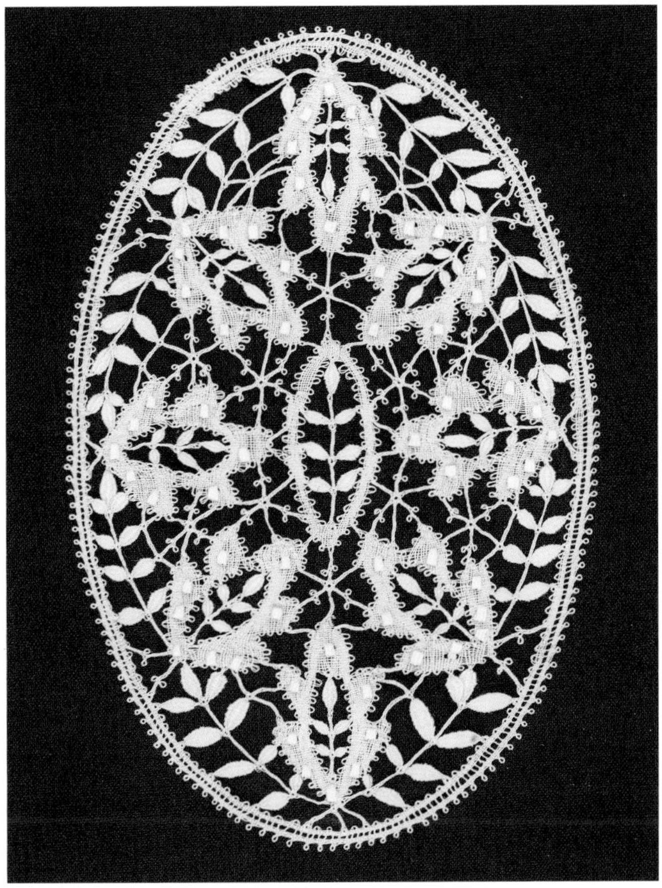

This is a slightly finer design that is worked in a finer thread. It has a vein on the outside edge trail formed by twisting the workers on every row. Raised and rolled tallies on the leaves add to the texture of the lace.

23

FEATHERED LEAF

This pattern was inspired by a painting by a local artist with a history of relatives and ancestors working in the Nottingham lace industry. Victoria Brown very kindly gave permission for her painting to be included in this book and as the inspiration for the design.

This painting is from Victoria's 'Losing Lace Series' of paintings. It is called 'Levers Feathered Leaf', and it was inspired by a sample from a 1930s lace pattern book that belonged to her great grandfather, Thomas Stocks. It is painted in oils, gold leaf and includes machine lace on canvas.

This demonstrates how you can design new lace patterns using inspiration from a range of sources. Ensure you seek permission from the artist before you use their work in a design.

http://www.victoriabrownart.com
for more about Victoria.

Made in Presencia Finca 60, approximately 100 pairs.

This design might look slightly repetitive, but there is so much shape and movement in it that no two leaf fronds are quite the same. This variety makes the pattern more interesting to work.

Note that outside the outlining trail the leaf fronds have picots, while inside it they do not.

24

WISTERIA

Many of the designs in this book feature flower motifs, and this one is included as a personal tribute to an outstanding summer flower. There is something very enthralling about Wisteria flowers. They signal the start of summer.

Made in Presencia Finca 60,
approximately 100 pairs.

The pattern is worked from the top, as it is viewed, so the challenging part of the leaves is worked first. Start with the right hand leaf, and in order to join across the leaf, several points are started at the same time. The left hand leaf, with the downward direction of the leaf, is much easier to work. As with previous patterns, where elements of the design 'grow' outside the frame of the piece, the leaves have picots outside the frame but none on the inside.

25

PAISLEY MOTIF

This design was taken from a parasol in the private collection of Laurie Waters. She kindly granted her permission for the design to be used for this purpose and published in this book.

The parasol is 27" in diameter. From studying the photographs, it appears to have been worked in sections. The centre has been worked as one piece, the motifs worked separately and then joined with the ground, with the edge frill attached after working. It can be seen in the photographs that the edging is a different shade to the rest of the parasol.

The paisley motif was a particularly attractive area of the design. As it appeared to have been made separately, it was quite easily extracted and worked as a motif. This photograph shows the back of the lace, and a join can be clearly seen on the right hand side of the edge.

Made in Presencia Finca 60, approximately 90+ pairs.

The motif worked particularly well. Although this is the most difficult pattern in the book, all the pairs are correctly placed to work successfully around the holes in the cloth. Some experience of working holes in cloth is needed before attempting this pattern. It is not easy to work multiple holes at the same time, and you need to focus on which hole belongs where. It is hugely beneficial to colour in your pricking before you start to work it, as there are many pairs on the pillow!

Photograph showing holes in cloth, with twisted pairs across the holes.

Note that the points of the cloth stitch have a plait connection to feed the central cloth stitch. This helps move pairs to the correct place where they are needed.

The original also uses a gimp outline that was not used in this modern version. Whether or not you use a gimp outline is up to you.

Photograph shows multiple holes in cloth at the bottom of the motif.

If you are using the correct thickness of thread, and if your pairs come in where they should, everything should fall into place. There is a distinct character and feel about working a design that originates from the 19th century, and this one was something special to work. Perhaps one day the whole parasol will become a pattern to work.

Additional patterns

These additional patterns are offered for interpretation and working without instructions.

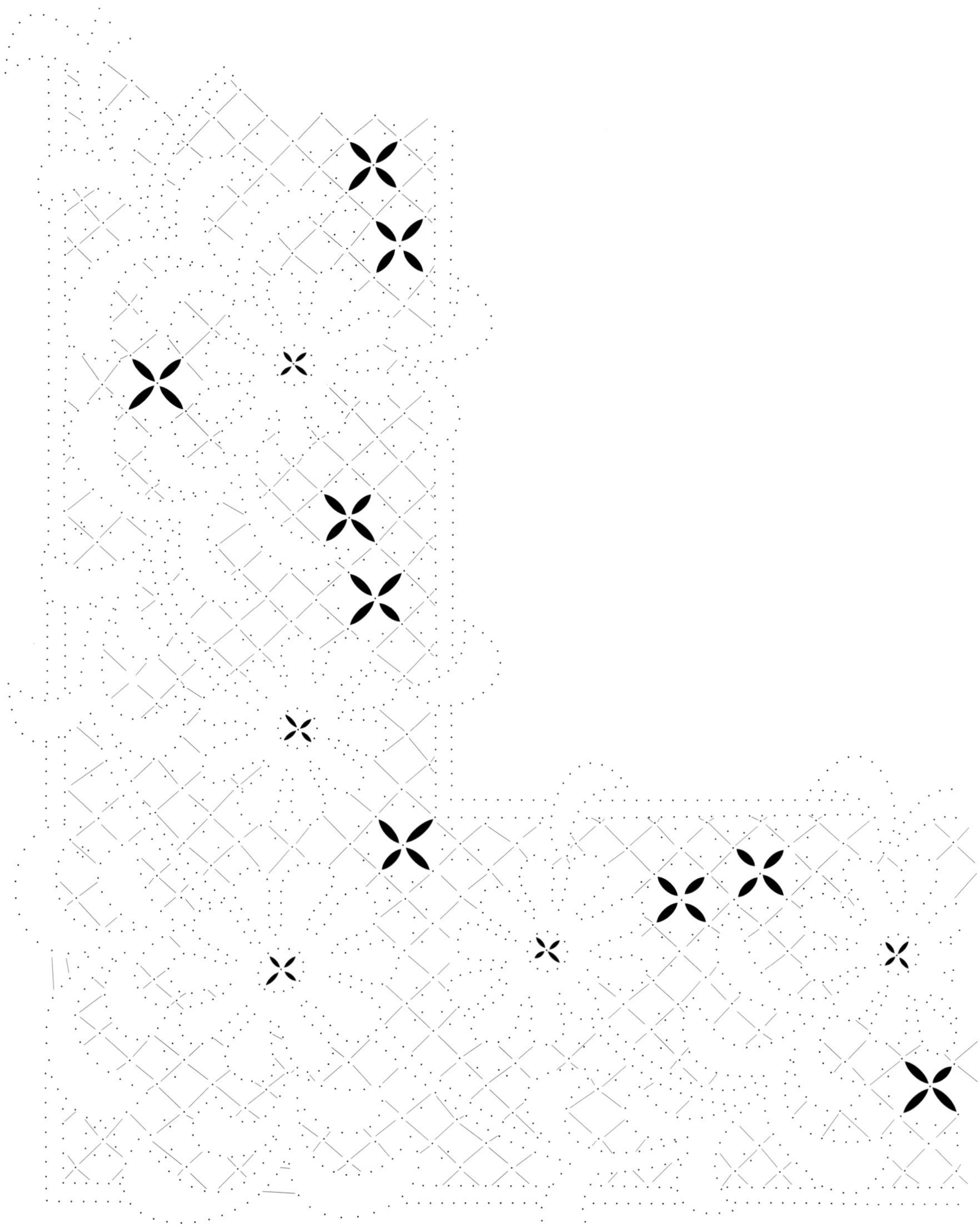

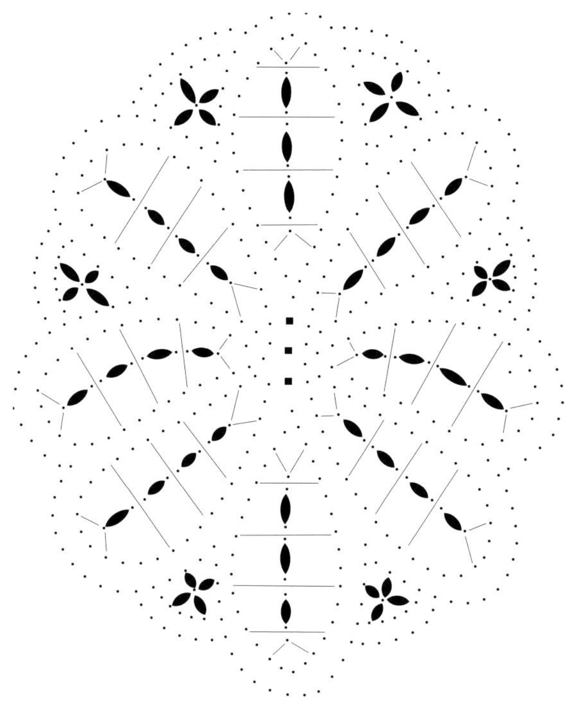

INDEX